LOST IN FRANCE

From the bars of France to England's press calls along the way, Christian Smyth had unique access to the nation's players and journalists as they careered round France '98. Not so much 'All Played Out' as 'A Bit Hard Done By', England's end-of-term report will read: 'Should have done better'. For the players, punters and pundits, this is how it was . . .

Since graduating from Bradford University in 1989, Christian Smyth has been a senior editor of *The Big Issue*, *Loaded* and *Eat Soup*. He has recently edited *FourFourTwo* and written for *The Times*, *The Observer* and *GQ*. He is working on his first novel.

LOST IN FRANCE

Frontline Dispatches from World Cup '98

CHRISTIAN SMYTH

MAINSTREAM
PUBLISHING

EDINBURGH AND LONDON

First published in Great Britain in 1998 by
MAINSTREAM PUBLISHING COMPANY
(EDINBURGH) LTD
7 Albany Street
Edinburgh EH1 3UG

ISBN 1 84018 097 8

A CIP catalogue record for this book is available
form the British Library

Typeset in Bembo
Printed in Great Britain by Butler & Tanner Ltd

Contents

	Acknowledgements	9
1.	'Tickets, buy or sell'	11
2.	Touchdown	14
3.	Michael Owen	24
4.	England expects	40
5.	The boy Beckham	52
6.	Port of storm	62
7.	The morning after	82
8.	The trouble with David . . .	89
9.	Time for some answers	104
10.	Hoddle's French connection	110
11.	Ghost town	116
12.	Now we're getting somewhere	123
13.	A weekend in Paris	136
14.	Journey's end	147
15.	The longest day	161
16.	Tee hee and sympathy	177
17.	The final verdict	184

Acknowledgements

I'd like to thank all my friends and family for their encouragement during the writing of this book. I'd also like to thank Richard Kerry for doing the cover, the Cashmore clan for collecting the gumph, Mr Terry for the many lunches and the inspired title suggestions, Simon Kanter at *FourFourTwo* for sending me to France in the first place, Judy at Mainstream for reading the script, Dan, Scott, Ginger Paul, Hedge and Marcela for the capers in France, and last but not least Mikey, for the kind words and warm heart when I was far away and feeling lonely. Cheers.

I would also like to thank Scott Morgan at *FourFourTwo* magazine for permission to reproduce some of the material in Chapter Three.

'Only one team is going to win it now . . .'
Kevin Keegan, 22 June 1998

CHAPTER ONE

'Tickets, buy or sell'

Deep in the bowels of the Stade de France a cartoon character stood in front of a mass of cameras, his goofy teeth lit up by the light of a thousand flashbulbs. His yellow shirt glared beneath the creation of a halo above his head and he seemed to suffer in silence the indignity of being jostled and tugged. It was like watching a mugging, but that crime would happen much later.

For now the wonderful stadium on the outskirts of Paris reverberated to the sound of Brazilian samba and Celtic pipes. We were at the 1998 World Cup finals and right now, at centre stage, was the star of the show. Ladies and gentlemen, we give you Ronaldo! And he was here to cement his reputation as the greatest player in football.

Ronaldo had been given some bright new boots by his sponsor, Nike. They looked pretty good with Nike's bright new Brazilian shirts that every soccer-mad Parisian tourist would be wearing over the next month.

Blue with a silver lining, the boots weren't dissimilar to the £120 footwear sported by fashion-conscious clubbers in Britain. Was this an omen?

Brazil probably didn't fancy playing Scotland for their opening match. The Scots may not have much of a record in the World Cup finals but, like all the weaker nations in the tournament, they could play to the stereotype, a cliché that suggested they'd be tricky customers who'd put up a fight and might sneak something at set-pieces.

The eve of the game had seen Paris overwhelmed by the invasion of thousands of angry 'bridge and tunnel people' as *Le Figaro* described them the following morning. These suburban demonstrators came to disrupt the opening ceremonies in the streets the night before kick-off because, it seemed, they had a grievance with the amount of money being set aside for football instead of houses.

There were one or two arrests. Sadly Stan Collymore wasn't amongst them, but he got dealt with in time-honoured fashion by a Scotsman. If you beat up Ulrika Jonsson, the least you deserve is a headbutt.

In the bars around the Bastille, Scotland supporters in the uniform of kilt and Brazil shirt drank the first of many cities dry and encouraged the locals to get into the spirit of *le Coupe du Monde*. Bemused Parisians looked on as grown men, affable but drunk, went in search of wine, women and tickets. I was offered six hundred pounds for mine by a man in his fifties who told me he would 'go off tae the cashpoint and get me ma money!'. I wisnae selling.

We mingled with a couple of Argentinians and played football in the streets. I asked one Scot whether Rangers and Celtic fans ever got together.

'Never,' he said. 'These lads are all Aberdeen and Dundee. The only time you'll get bother with Scotland is when the Old Firm gang up. But there's no trouble here.'

One *rue* had been turned into a part of Paris that will forever ring to the sound of bagpipes as bar after bar overflowed with members of the Tartan Army. A group of Brazilians wandered by and received a round of applause. Anticipation and excitement hung in the air.

Next day, the train ride up to St Denis took fifteen minutes from the centre of town. Like all foreign cities, Paris looked large on the map, but after a few days the layout of the Metro was easy to handle and distances shortened. The trains never stopped running, and if there was a hold-up, there was always a pretty lady around to show you the way if you asked nicely. I liked Paris, and it seemed to agree with me.

The area around the gigantic, 80,000-seater stadium swelled with people. They were mainly Brazilians and Scots, but there were Mexicans, Italians and Chileans there too.

The touts were all English.

'Got any spares? Any spares?'

'Buy or sell.'

The ruthless nastiness that is a tattooed Englishman with sunburn and scruffy clothing set the tone for many an encounter along the way, but not even the presence of a few of the 'lads' could take away the magnificence of the occasion.

Amongst the thugs, the police, the children and the hot-dog vendors were thousands of football fans. One group had come straight off the plane from Rio on a promise of tickets and spent the duration of the match arguing their right to enter with a nonplussed *gendarme* at the gate. They were still there when the rain came down on the stroke of full-time.

As I plonked myself among the gentlemen of Her Majesty's press and took in the sight of Frenchmen on stilts, overgrown babies throwing balls in the air and people with little sense dangling by a thread from the roof of the stadium, my heart pounded to the beat of the drum and bass that accompanied this, the greatest of opening ceremonies. I was there at the start of the sixteenth World Cup, France '98 . . . and for myself and England's footballers, this is how it was.

CHAPTER TWO

Touchdown

The town of La Baule rests on the north-west Atlantic coast of France. Blessed with its climate, it is Brittany's answer to the Riviera. The England squad enjoyed staying here when they won *Le Tournoi* in 1996. Concrete hotels, designed to look like hands outstretched towards the ocean, are interspersed with palm trees along the front, while posh villas nestle in the tiny streets behind. In the summer the population swells from fourteen thousand to a hundred and fifty thousand. It's the quaint old-fashioned nature of the place that attracts visitors, who come here mainly from Paris – that and the five miles of golden sand that make up one of the longest beaches in Europe, according to the brochure.

You can feel the money here as you saunter past the boutiques selling Armani and Gucci. Even the poodles are clipped and powdered.

La Baule has thirty-eight sports clubs, two football stadiums, three tennis clubs and an international golf club. It is also the summer destination of international celebrities like Mel Gibson and Joan Collins. No wonder the England players felt at home.

Base camp would be the Golf de Saint-Denac hotel on the outskirts of town. For the purposes of training, England had commandeered the local football pitch used by a junior school, ringed off for the exclusive use of the squad. Representatives from the FA had already been in town appeasing the locals who were proud to look after the English but a little put out by the demands for seclusion. T-shirts, balls and signed photos made up for common courtesy. The England set-up was very different from that of some of the other countries taking part in the World Cup. Brazil, for instance, had food stalls, a samba band and seats for a thousand spectators, and encouraged their players to talk to the media. Norway, who were based just up the road from England, allowed press and players to mingle freely in the hotel lobby. Team England, in contrast, would be operating behind closed doors.

The squad flew in from Caen on Tuesday, 9 June, arriving at Nantes-Atlantique airport at 9.15 p.m. after a half-hour delay, and headed straight for the hotel. As the delegation of fifty (bringing with it four tons of luggage) got off the plane in the rain, Glenn Hoddle was the only one to comment. 'We all enjoyed the flight,' he said.

Earlier, the players had taken on Caen, a side in the French Second Division, winning 1–0 in a match played behind closed doors away from the prying eye of the camera. Local dignitaries were invited to watch the match by the club and it was to them that journalists turned for news of the team formation. A great deal was made of the fact that Michael Owen had partnered Alan Shearer up front and that Tottenham's Darren Anderton, who had barely been fit enough to play a full ninety minutes of football a month before, had replaced Manchester United's David Beckham on the right side of midfield.

That match was Hoddle's first chance to see how the team was shaping up. He had given the players a short break after warm-up games in Morocco and encouraged them to see their families and have a rest. One young man went home to mum and dad and played a round of golf while another was photographed with a blonde on one arm and a fag in his mouth after a night on the tiles at the Babylon Club in Portugal. They were both vying for the same position in the team but, while Michael Owen was raw, young and supremely talented, Teddy Sheringham was experienced and thought to be Alan Shearer's preferred partner. Hoddle had already dumped Paul Gascoigne from the squad for failing to take responsibility for his fitness (Gazza had been caught drinking during a round of golf on the day the final twenty-two-man squad for France was announced) and many thought Sheringham was lucky to escape with just a poorly phrased – and barely believable – public apology. When you remembered Hoddle's opinion that in life you 'don't get mad, you get even', you didn't fancy being in Teddy's shoes.

England held their first training session the following after-noon, Wednesday, 10 June. The players worked out to techno music broadcast for seventy-five minutes from two speakers on the side of the pitch. Ian Wright might not have made it to France but the lingering presence of his taste in music was keeping the team going.

Gary Neville and Les Ferdinand sat on the sidelines for this first session with a reported calf injury and a damaged Achilles tendon respectively.

Hoddle had expressed his concern with the state of the pitch a few weeks before England had arrived. He'd brought in gardeners from Wembley Stadium to tend to the green stuff and had left orders for eight different types of pitch surface to be drawn out using a grid on the grass. On arrival it was reported that Hoddle and Shearer judged the pitch to be excellent but the impression of monocled commandants at parade ground inspection was hard to shake off. There was much eyebrow-raising among the locals. 'Maybe with your football and passion for techno music we're not so different after all,' mocked one member of the press.

★

As the rain hammered down on to the huge awning of the roof at the Stade de France, Charlie Nicholas and Joe Jordan sought refuge from the scrum of journalists running this way and that, a bit like lost ants. Or headless chickens. The two former Scotland internationals were shorter than you might expect for a pair of forwards and Charlie looked like the good times were beginning to catch up on him. But they looked happy.

Craig Brown, on the other hand, was furious. He'd been giving the Scotland defence a rollicking for fifteen minutes on account of the sloppy early goal from a corner they'd allowed through and then the heartbreaking own goal from Tommy Boyd in the second half. This, after stout defending by Colin Hendry (including one magnificent moment where he trapped the ball on his left thigh then juggled it twice on either foot as he made his way up the pitch, much to the delight of the crowd). The yellow-haired leader of the Scots had performed miracles to keep the score respectable but you sensed the Brazilian genius of Ronaldo had dazzled only occasionally by his standards. Still, as one Scottish fan on the RER express train back to Paris put it later in the night, 'When is it ever going to be our turn? When are we going to have our day?'

Before we left the stadium, a pack of Japanese pressmen legged it up the station stairs in pursuit of a shaggy-haired fellow with a craggy face but no cigar. It was Cesar Menotti, the genius behind Argentina's 1978 World Cup triumph and a man not usually so relaxed without a cigarette to his lips. He was a walking billboard promoting every good reason to give up the weed. If death in the guise of the Grim Reaper walked on two legs and hailed from South America then Menotti was your man. He was a legend, though, and even if legends were two-a-penny round here on the opening day of the World Cup, he was king of legends.

★

To get accredited for the *Coupe du Monde* my fellow journalists and I had to apply to the FA, wait for their acquiesence back in January and then dispatch a massive bundle of forms (*formulaire d'accréditation pour la presse écrite*), passport photos and money (three hundred quid) to the French Organising Committee, known henceforth as the CFO – at the Crédit Agricole, Paris, Ile de France. Along with this package we had to state which first-round games we wanted to see. We were told that on no account could we go to more than one game per day. (As if anyone would in a place the size of France.) I duly filled in all the England games and then planned out a route that would allow me to watch as many games featuring Brazil, Argentina, France, Holland and Italy as possible given the problems of getting around France and the time it takes to do so. (I say problems not because the infrastructure is poor – it is in fact very good and the TGV high-speed trains are a godsend – but because the French capacity for strikes is bettered by no other European country; Air France pilots were at it up till kick-off for the opening game.)

★

During the run-up to the opening match of the tournament, it became clear that there was a problem with tickets. British reports and French TV had indicated that France would keep sixty per cent of all the tickets, while the rest were split down to twenty per cent for the media and twenty per cent for the official sponsors. The sixty-four matches in the France '98 programme entailed mounting the biggest ticketing operation ever seen in France: 2,500,000 tickets, and revenue from ticket sales accounted for more than fifty per cent of organising costs for the 1998 World Cup.

The CFO intended to make France '98 accessible to the largest number of people. They felt this was evident from what they laughingly called a 'friendly pricing policy': 500,000 tickets at less than FF150 (that's about fifteen pounds) and one ticket in two at FF250 or less. 'Ticketing sales have been a great success,' said Michel Platini and Fernand Sastre, presidents of the organising committee. (Sastre sadly died on the eve of England's match with Tunisia.)'The tickets were all sold within a few months when we had anticipated sales going on until February 1998. We were able to count on the largest distribution and information network ever mounted in France for a single ticket sales operation. The CFO's technological partners involved in the organisation and setting up of this ticket operation have reason to be proud of themselves.' As anyone who tried will know, getting hold of one of these precious tickets was nigh on impossible – even the FA had trouble increasing England's allocation after the first round. The French players complained after the match against Croatia that there wasn't any atmosphere in the Stade de France, simply because most of what Didier Deschamps described as the 'real fans' couldn't get in. Indeed, the final irony may be that it was the hosts' supporters who suffered most from the gluttony of corporatism.

On the eve of the opening game, the CFO released a statement regarding the ticket fiasco: 'During the last few days, the CFO has received numerous letters and telephone calls from companies and individuals who have been the victims of unacceptable business practices on the part of certain agencies both in France and abroad.

'Certain unscrupulous agents have undertaken to sell tickets for World Cup matches in sometimes unbelievable quantities, which they are now unable to hand over to their buyers – especially for the "big" matches (such as the opener, the third-place play-off and the final), and matches of particular interest in the first round, such as the game between Belgium and the Netherlands. In an attempt to render their own position easier or to extricate themselves entirely, these agents are now trying to thrust responsibility onto the shoulders of the CFO and FIFA by claiming that both of them are holding back a large number of tickets. There is not a shred of truth in these assertions.

'In the face of this unacceptable situation, the CFO is continuing to co-operate with the authorities of the various nations concerned. Among other things, this has resulted in the cessation of activity of the company "Great Portland Entertainments" in England.

'For several months now, the CFO has been warning buyers to be on their guard, and regrets that *not everybody has heeded its numerous warnings.*

'The CFO utterly condemns the practices of certain tourist agents, who are guilty at the very least of unacceptable irresponsibility, or, in the most serious cases, of actions which may well incur legal proceedings. It is incomprehensible, for instance, that a well-informed professional agency would even consider buying tickets from the Cameroon Federation representing up to 15 per cent of the stadium capacity for matches which do not involve the national team of that country.

'The CFO wishes to emphasise that it has no connection with these agencies, and appreciates the immense disappointment of supporters who have been swindled in this way. The CFO will be instigating all legal proceedings needful to protect the interests of the World Cup, and also invites the victims of such malpractice to undertake all civil and legal action necessary against the agencies concerned.

'With only a few hours to go before the World Cup kicks off, the CFO and the authorities of the various countries involved are redoubling their vigilance. Apart from the numerous preventative measures undertaken by the CFO, several checking methods have been instigated and a number of prosecutions are already under way. Recently the CFO carried out a search in the home of an individual convicted of reselling tickets on the black market. The tickets still in the possession of this buyer were seized and all the tickets, including those which had been resold, were cancelled.'

So that's clear then. The ticketing fiasco was absolutely nothing to do with the French organisers – indeed, if you'd read the label properly, you'd have been all right, and for those who were *swindled* the organisers appreciate your *immense disappointment* but can do nothing more to help. Bless 'em.

★

Back in La Baule, the players were holding forth at lunch on the first day, as Brazil and Scotland warmed up on the pitch in Paris. Michael Owen wandered in looking relaxed and quietly confident in his regulation Umbro polo shirt and poolsiders. When pushed, he admitted that the Shearer-Sheringham partnership up front was the most likely starting combination in four days' time. Finishing the sentence with a lingering 'maybe' just kept us on our toes.

Later in the week, Owen, who has the lowest handicap in the squad, was lined up to play golf alongside Paul Scholes against the leading strike duo. At the training camp in La Manga during the final build-up to the World Cup, England's SAS partnership had put one over the young pretenders and Owen made it clear he was out for revenge. 'Ask my family how bad I am at losing,' said the eighteen-year-old. 'I think it's a quality – Alan Shearer has it too.' There was no mention of Teddy.

Gareth Southgate had vowed for two years that he would never take another penalty for England. Until now. Southgate, who had cruelly missed his spot-kick against Germany in the Euro '96 semi-final, swore that he would never go through another of the scenarios that has plagued him since then. But now he was looking forward to the opening match against Tunisia and said: 'I've thought about it a lot, as you would expect. I never thought I would take another penalty. But I will if I'm needed. Let's face it, a match would have to go to sudden death because I'm not first choice among the penalty-takers!'

After the infamous miss against Germany, the Aston Villa centre-back just wanted to forget all about it, but he eventually succumbed and agreed to do a pizza advert with other England miss-hits, Stuart Pearce and Chris Waddle. Assessing things now, days before the opening fixture, he made it clear that time was proving a great healer and that he was less troubled now by the events at Wembley in 1996. 'I'd rather concentrate on 90 minutes or 120 minutes of an upcoming match than think of something that has taken just ten seconds in my fifteen-year career,' he said. 'I could go on for ever talking about it, but there is nothing I can do to change what happened. Although that incident will always rankle with me, I don't think I have anything to prove.'

Southgate spoke of his belief that even if they didn't win the World Cup, England would finish top of the fair-play league – something they managed in Italia '90. 'We're a bit too honest at times,' he explained. 'Other teams act like basketball players and go down for a foul at the merest touch. But I think it's appalling to try and get an opponent sent off. We would all be choked if we missed an important match through suspension.

'We won't be upset either by the appointment of a hard-line referee. We'd sooner have a stronger man in control, and not somebody who is easily influenced.'

Southgate believed England would be a force in this World Cup, despite all the criticism generated by their substandard build-up. 'The results over the last couple of years means we have become respected again. You can take it from me that the players are completely focused on the job in hand.

'Our group is very similar to that in Euro '96 and I have the feeling we are more optimistic than we were before that tournament. The expectation levels throughout the squad are higher now. And we know we are playing for the nation.'

And as for Hoddle's preference for 3–5–2 over the traditional 4–4–2?

'With the three at the back, we can be more flexible in our approach to matches,' he replied. 'Our defensive record is very good, despite the age-old criticism that we look shaky at the back.'

No one could argue with that. And in four days' time we'd see if he was right.

CHAPTER THREE

Michael Owen

Picture the scene. It's 4 July 1990 and Michael Owen is plonked in front of the telly in his parents' house in Hawarden, Flintshire. Slumped between his two elder brothers on the sofa, he drags himself up to the edge of his seat for a better view. It's getting on for ten o'clock and, like most kids his age, he should be in bed. But his dad, Terry, the former Everton player, recognises the significance of the moment, and for one night only little Michael is allowed to stay up.

The semi-final of the World Cup is eventually settled by a penalty shoot-out. As English hopes are blasted over the bar and a nation sheds its tears, comedians twiddle with early workings of plays like *An Evening with Gary Lineker*, but Michael Owen's night has come to a depressing end. He is tucked up in bed and drifts off to sleep.

Eight years on, and Michael Owen has jettisoned the pyjamas for an England shirt. He is the first to be introduced to a reverential press pack when he steps off the coach from England's exclusive Golf de Saint-Menac hotel and they can't wait to shake his hand. This is the man many, including the Italian national coach Cesare Maldini and Pelé no less, are tipping to emerge as the star of France

'98. (When Pelé was asked who he fancied to do well this summer, he replied: 'I like the look of that Michael Owen, he's my favourite Manchester United player.')

He's about as tall as you'd expect (around five foot eight) but more solid, with square shoulders and a neck that would sit well on a prop-forward – though not one as quick as this kid.

Owen used to box as a child; his dad thought it might help him look after himself, but he plays down his pugilistic past, claiming, probably justifiably, that journalists have read too much into it. So how does someone of his diminutive stature compete when they're up against some of the best defenders in the world?

'Sometimes you might look at someone and think, yeah, he's too strong or too quick, anything like that. When I see a big defender I think, great, he can't turn.'

Owen's fan mail averaged around a hundred letters a week before the World Cup. By now it's up to three hundred. Everyone wants a slice of the wonder kid. His mum still deals with most of the letters but coping with the attention he gets when out in public is something he's had to handle on his own. 'I think at the start you quite like it. It's quite nice having people come up to you and say "You're Michael Owen, aren't you?".'

He tells the story of when he and Liverpool team-mate Danny Murphy were coming back from training and popped in to the local McDonald's. 'We were only there to pick something up quickly and we just got mobbed. We were in there an hour and a quarter signing autographs.' Owen shakes his head. 'Never again.'

★

'Go on, Michael, hit it!' yells Steve McManaman. Owen runs onto one of those perfectly clipped passes he's been getting from his team-mate all season at Liverpool. Glenn Hoddle is standing just off to the side looking on as the curly-haired playmaker does everything he can to urge the eighteen-year-old on. Hoddle and McManaman fell out over Macca's insistence on having surgery last summer – the manager had wanted him to play at *Le Tournoi* – but he's the one that's making Owen tick on the training-ground. Hoddle may have cause to be grateful by the end of the summer if Owen begins to shine.

★

Owen always knew he was going to be a star. Since the age of seven he's been the best player in every team he's played for. At eight he was already a minor celebrity, the local papers running stories of his goalscoring feats. When he turned up at the county trials he was the only player whose name everyone knew already.

Apart from a two-year spell at Lilleshall, Owen has lived in Wales all his life. Although born in Chester he went to school in Wales and played his first ever organised football match on a Welsh pitch. Owen's team, Mold Alexander Under-10s, won that game, overcoming Bagillt 2–0.

Early in 1998 Owen and his ever first manager, Howard Roberts, gave these revealing interviews to *FourFourTwo* magazine. According to Roberts, Owen had scored thirty-four goals in twenty-four starts that season. 'In one match he scored nine goals,' recalls Roberts. 'And that was in the first twenty minutes. I didn't think it was fair on the other team so I made him go in goal for the rest of the game. Do you know what he did? He sat on the edge of the box complaining that no one was giving him any back-passes.'

Owen was only allowed to play for Mold after his mum wrote a letter to the club consenting to his selection. At the time, county rules stipulated that a kid had to be at least eight to play in the Under-10s; Owen was only seven.

Against teams with big kids at the back he was occasionally taken off for his own protection, but not once did he request to be substituted. 'He got flattened a few times,' says Roberts, 'but it never bothered him. He just laughed it off and got on with it.'

Despite his size, Owen was always played at centre-forward. Such was his instinct and awareness of the position that Roberts claimed he had no option but to pick him there. What impressed most was his ability to run off the ball, something that in later years helped make up Glenn Hoddle's mind that Owen was ready for a place in the squad for France; while his team-mates charged into the box cavalry-style, Owen would delay his run until precisely the right moment, inevitably meeting the ball first when it arrived. In addition, his capacity for running at speed with the ball was evident even then.

'Obviously Michael had a lot of pace,' says Roberts. 'And when he ran with the ball he appeared to dance. I've seen him run forty yards without seeming to touch it. He always knew just how far ahead to put the ball so he didn't have to break his stride.'

After one season at Mold Alexandra, Owen was invited to a trial for Deeside primary schools. At eight he was selected to play for the Under-11s. Tales of his scoring exploits for Deeside are legion; in two seasons for the Under-11 side he hit ninety-seven goals (the previous record, set by former Anfield legend, Ian Rush, was seventy-two).

By the time Owen was eleven just about every club in the country had their eye on him. There's a story about Brian Kidd coming to check him out at one of his games. Kidd was on the touchline and mentioned to one of Owen's coaches that he'd seen the boy a couple of times and thought he had great potential but hadn't thought much of his first-half performance. Kidd was persuaded to hang around and in the second half Deeside went on to win 6–0, Owen scoring all six. United wanted to take him there and then but FA regulations restricting travelling distances for boys in his age group put the end to that. Despite spending a couple of weeks deciding which club to join on schoolboy forms (he'd checked out Arsenal and Nottingham Forest), his heart was already set on going to Anfield.

As a youngster Owen was a rabid Evertonian. His childhood idol was Gary Lineker. So why did he choose Liverpool? 'I could have signed for Everton,' he reveals. 'But I was at Liverpool from an early age. I liked the staff and got to know all the players and really felt part of the set-up. There was never really any chance I would go anywhere else.'

Owen cites Steve Heighway's role as the most crucial in his decision – not because of anything Liverpool's youth development officer said or taught him, but rather for what he gave him: no matter how important the fixture Heighway always saw Owen right for match tickets and supplied him with new boots when he needed them. 'Just the little things that keep you happy,' says Owen.

It's his father who exerts the greatest influence over his career, though. The two are almost inseparable; Terry has attended virtually every game Owen has played since he was seven.

Terry Owen was a professional footballer too. After making his début for Everton at eighteen in 1968 he went on to play for a number of league clubs before winding down his career in non-league football. 'I'd like to think I've helped him a wee bit,' he told the *Chester Chronicle*. 'But Michael's progress has been all down to his great mental strength. He was born with ability and has made good use of it.'

As well as being his son's staunchest supporter, Terry Owen is also his fiercest critic. If his boy has a bad game he'll let him know it – but not by ranting and raving; Owen senior prefers the silent treatment, often refusing to speak to Michael after matches in which he considers his son to have underperformed.

It doesn't happen often. After demolishing Rush's record for Deeside, Michael went on to break the England schoolboy record for the most number of goals in a season, scoring twelve of his country's twenty goals in 1995–96. (That same season he also found time to pass all his GCSEs.)

On his début for England Under-18s in 1996–97 he scored all four goals against Northern Ireland, then shot Liverpool to their first ever FA Youth Cup victory with eleven goals in five games, including a hat-trick in the semi-final against holders Manchester United. In May 1997 he made his senior début for Liverpool, scoring their only goal in a 2–1 defeat at Wimbledon; last season, at the age of eighteen, he became the youngest full England international this century, was voted the PFA's Young Player of the Year and finished joint top scorer in the Premiership with eighteen goals. He is also the proud owner of a Blue Peter badge, awarded to him when he appeared on the show as a fifteen-year-old.

Asked about the World Cup, he asserted that 'Brazil are probably going to start favourites but we're not going there looking to come second. We're going there to win.'

And would he be happy sitting on the bench, seeing as he's only eighteen?

'No, I don't think anyone's happy sat on the bench. When I got into the Liverpool squad I wasn't happy being sub. And when I got into the first team I wasn't happy not playing for England. I don't think you can ever be satisfied as a player unless you're in the starting eleven.'

A few months ago, word was that Hoddle didn't fancy him – a feeling intensified when the England manager was widely quoted criticising Owen's off-pitch behaviour. 'When I saw it in the paper I didn't know what was happening,' recalls Owen. 'There was no clue the story was going to be in there. I just woke up and saw my face on the front page.'

Later that morning he got a phone call from Hoddle. 'He told me he had been talking about the dangers to young players in general and it had been taken out of context.' It was an explanation Owen was happy with.

More difficult to fathom was Hoddle's observation that Owen is not a 'natural goalscorer'. The manager has subsequently said that he was misquoted on this subject, too, claiming what he meant was that Owen is not just a goalscorer but also a creator of goals. Indeed he is but, that said, it is the role of goalscorer that he performs more 'naturally'.

'As a striker you've always got to be an optimist. You've always got to think if he misses, if I can get in there, or if he runs there I can run in his space – always looking for an opportunity to get in. If there's a through ball on, you make the run.'

And if you don't get it?

'You make another.'

Missed chances play on his mind. Often he goes to bed thinking about what he might have done differently. Against Chile on his England début he had an early chance and went for the near post. 'I've thought about that a few times,' he rues. 'At the time I thought maybe I should have smacked it but, looking at the replay, I think it would have got blocked by someone running in. I'm not sure what I could have done differently. Sometimes it just happens like that.'

Every striker has a dream goal, a fantasy strike. Owen is no different . . . except that *his* dream goal is already a reality. 'Do you want me to describe it to you?' he pleads. 'It was for England schoolboys against Scotland,' he begins. 'They'd just equalised and we were about to take a centre-kick. From the kick-off my strike partner passed it to me and I started to run. I can't remember how many players I beat but it was a lot, most of the team. When I got to the edge of the box I just smashed it. It flew into the top corner between the angle of post and cross-bar.'

Now his dream was merely to repeat it – preferably in the World Cup finals . . .

★

We'd been standing outside the gate at England's delightful training headquarters for over an hour on an early morning in February. We were cold, tired and in need of something special to cheer us up. It was one of those bristling winter mornings where the sunshine belies the fact that you should be feeling miserable. But something was happening today that made even the most embittered tabloid journalist optimistic, nay cheerful. Michael Owen.

Owen's so fast and so short that he gets round the training-pitch like a kid on a broomstick. There was something magical about the hold he had on the banks of photographers who queued up and greedily snapped off the pictures that would be landing on our breakfast tables the following morning.

The country had a new star, a player who, at eighteen years and fifty-eight days was about to become the youngest player this century to play for England. Hoddle had picked the Liverpool prodigy for the Wembley fixture with Chile on 11 February 1998. The nation, as they say, expected.

When Roy Evans, Owen's club manager, was asked to assess his striker's World Cup chances he told the press he thought the teenager was ready. Behind him stood a queue of pundits eager to punt the same line. Owen hadn't yet kicked a ball at full-international level and in six months had picked up his first Under-18, Under-21 and now senior caps. Was there nothing he couldn't do?

With Alan Shearer just back from injury, Les Ferdinand still on the Tottenham casualty bench and Ian Wright and Robbie Fowler going through lean spells, not to mention the demise of Stan Collymore at Villa, Owen was suddenly in contention. A brilliant winner on the previous Sunday afternoon against Newcastle sealed the decision in Hoddle's mind and the teenager was in.

It was no secret that Evans thought the lad could handle the pressure. He believed Glenn Hoddle was considering Owen and pointed out that Hoddle had been to see the lad play quite frequently of late. The weight of expectation was obvious and cynics doubted Owen's ability to cope with the pressure but one thing was certain – Liverpool football club was backing his claim. He was playing every match and he was playing for his England place. Evans praised the single-mindedness of the player and pointed out that nothing fazed him. It was clear that Evans felt there was much more to come.

Evans had bought the hugely experienced German international, Karl-Heinz Riedle, a European Cup-winner with Borussia Dortmund the previous season, to partner Fowler up front, with Owen expected to come off the bench and push them for a place. But the prodigy was keeping the German out of the side. 'From what we had seen from Michael at the end of last season and in pre-season matches, we knew he was ready and was going to challenge for one of the striking positions,' said Evans in the press. 'We were forced to play him from the off because of Robbie's injury, but to be fair the lad has taken his chance brilliantly and made it difficult to leave him out. We still need to be aware of his age and the amount of games he's playing, but he seems to be getting away with it just fine. He's been looking tired towards the end of the last couple of games, but then he has dug deep and finished as strong as anybody.

'I've no qualms about him being called up for England. He's a young man who thrives on the ambition of playing for his country. He doesn't want to be held back, and I wouldn't stop him. It just needs a bit of common sense. We have a very good relationship with Glenn Hoddle. If Michael was called up and I felt he didn't need too much training, I would say to Glenn: "Fine, have him, but make sure you don't kill him." That should be the relationship between a club manager and an international coach.'

Owen was sure he could handle it as he told us later that morning. 'The pressure doesn't worry me because I have high hopes for myself which, with a bit of luck, will lead to me being involved with the full England squad for the World Cup finals.'

*

Alan Shearer was back in the England squad and, as you'd expect, the England captain was getting the most attention at the press conferences England conducted at Bisham Abbey.

Dion Dublin was finishing off his chat with the press boys; he looked happy just to be here and we all liked him for his charm, his smile and his jokes. But Shearer was serious. Newcastle were suffering a backlash from the controversy surrounding their FA Cup fixture with non-league side Stevenage, and Shearer was seen, alongside manager Kenny Dalglish, as the villain in the annual soap opera that is English knockout football. There were a few perfunctory congratulations on his return from the serious injury that he'd sustained in a pre-season tournament at Goodison Park and then it was on to business.

Could we win the World Cup?

'We've got as good as chance as any . . .'

Did he rate Michael Owen's chances of getting there?

'He's given himself every opportunity of pushing for a place . . .'

You get the picture. Say nothing.

As Shearer 'chatted', a murmur went up at the back as Hoddle came through the throng with his hands clasped on the shoulders of the boy wonder.

I looked back at Shearer who was sitting down and couldn't see what was going on behind the fifty or so reporters. He looked concerned, as if he was thinking, *Hang on a minute, fellas, I haven't finished yet.*

Hoddle led Owen up onto a bank of tables at the back of the hall and, although Shearer continued for a few minutes more, the desire to get a good seat for the eighteen-year-old's first England press call meant the captain's time was up. 'Sorry, Al. But we'd rather be over there.'

Owen was asked how he felt about getting the call so early and what went through his mind when he found out he was in the squad.

Steven Howard from *The Sun* demonstrated an extensive knowledge of stats and reeled off Owen's career in minute detail: number of goals, appearances, how he'd scored on his début at every level and so on. He wasn't so much asking questions and showing off. Owen stared at him with a mixture of interest and amazement on his face. Was that a grin I spotted? He seemed almost amused that a grown man could live his life so vicariously.

'I know a lot of people expect a lot from me and I hope I can live up to those expectations,' said Owen. 'You see what happens to other players who start off with a bang in their career only to fade away. But I'm not worried about myself. I'm confident enough to say that won't ever happen to me as long as I work hard to maintain my form and keep on scoring goals. Right now, the Liverpool team is the most important thing, but I want to do well for myself, for my own ambition and to prove to the manager and the fans that I am the man for the job. It's a big leap being with youth-team players one day and training with world-class players the next. But I'm part of the first-team squad now. I've adjusted and the players don't think of me any differently to anyone else in the squad.

'Some defenders are quite physical and I've taken a lot of punishment, but you just have to put up with it. That's the way some people defend and you have to live with that. The only answer is to stand up for yourself and answer them by sticking the ball in the back of the net. I don't see it as a big problem, really. You've got to remember, I am playing against grown men who've been in the game a long time and they know different ways to handle players they see as a threat.

'It's great to hear people link me with the full England squad. I'd love to go to France in the summer. But all I can do is carry on playing well in any game I play – and then hope I'm handed the chance!

'To compare me with Robbie is impossible at the moment. I would put Robbie up there with someone like Alan Shearer. He's as good a finisher as there is. I'm still learning the game and people like Robbie and Karl-Heinz offer me advice which I'm quick to listen to. They have proved themselves at the top over a period of time, while I'm just starting out.'

Hoddle sat by Owen's side and lapped up the maturity coming out of the youngster's mouth. I'd seen Owen give a few post-match interviews on TV and thought he'd spoken a lot of sense then, but here he had us in the palm of his hand. We, the British press, were simply stunned by how measured his answers were to our questions. And by the length of time he spent answering them.

Hoddle was conscious of the clamour for Owen to be promoted to the first team. 'He is very exciting. I know that he, like Rio Ferdinand, will be a hell of a player in five years' time. But I have four months. I have to decide whether they could do, in a World Cup, what they are doing in the Premiership. Those boys are no problem for 2002. But can one score goals and the other defend in a World Cup this summer? Sometimes you get four or five injuries and the situation is forced on you. The decision is made for you.

'Or you might say the boy is good enough anyway and I'll go with him. It also depends what your needs are. Take strikers. Do we go for subtle movement or do we want a bit of a battering ram? It all depends on how you are going to play. So the composition of my World Cup squad is very complex.

'Owen has the right temperament and what he is doing, week in week out, for Liverpool suggests he can get into the final World Cup twenty-two.

'Sometimes youngsters can be in awe of more experienced internationals, but he never looked out of place even on his first day training with England. He displayed a lot of maturity. There is a time to show them [top players] no respect, and that's in the ninety minutes of a football match. Sometimes you can be in awe of your opponents and your performance suffers, but Michael can do it.

'He suggests that he might get into the final twenty-two. But we have four or five months to find out. So, can he do what he is doing in the Premiership against the best defenders in the world? It's a different league, and he has not had that much experience in Europe ... there is a gap there, another hurdle he has to get over.'

For those of us lucky enough to be here to see the start of something special there was no doubt that Owen had what it took to go all the way. He was being smart, keeping his head down but saying just enough to emphasis that *he* thought he was good enough to go to the World Cup.

Owen sat there smiling and said, 'I am delighted to have been called up for the England squad. It is no secret that my ambitions have always been to play for Liverpool and England. At this stage of my career is it vital for me to stay fit, keep learning and keep my feet firmly on the floor.'

Alan Shearer felt the teenager was ready for the step up, even if he didn't appreciate his own press conferences being disturbed. 'Michael's a very special talent and he's had a tremendous start to his career – I just hope he doesn't get too much pressure placed on him. From what I've seen, he looks as though he can handle it and what he's done so far has been unbelievable. I got a decent look at him in the three games against us [Newcastle had just played Liverpool three times in the space of twenty-three days] and it was clear his pace is a huge asset to him. But what I've noticed is that he doesn't appear to be fazed by anything or anybody. If the manager gives him his chance I know he wouldn't let anybody down.'

Owen thought he was ready, and his age didn't seem to be an issue with him – even if it was for everybody else. 'I think I'm ready. I don't see myself as a young lad coming into the game, just as one of the lads at Liverpool, and that's how the rest of them see me too. And playing for England won't bother me. I'll relish the opportunity. I'm confident in my ability to do well, and I certainly don't think age comes into it – as the manager said, if you're good enough, you're old enough.'

'Michael plays with his head up,' explained Hoddle. 'Anybody who does that will score and create, and Michael does. Age doesn't come into it. He's here because of his talent. We've groomed him over the last couple of get-togethers and he feels at home already. He's got the right temperament and he's shown no signs that he can't handle it. I'm putting no pressure on the boy. He's in good form, he's been called up by his country but if he doesn't make the World Cup squad he's got another ten years of going to World Cups and European Championships. I don't want to put that burden on him now. I just want him to go out and express himself as he has done since he started playing football.

'There's no problem with his ability to make decisions on the pitch. He's a unique player. He's something you don't see, a striker who really attacks people with the ball, very direct and as quick with the ball at his feet as without it. If you've got somebody who can do that in the last third of the pitch – and he's proved he can in the Premiership – it's a huge asset. He'll be a star of the future – it doesn't take a genius to work that out. What we need to find out in a short period of time now is if he's ready for the World Cup.'

Sitting next to the England manager, enjoying the attention and speaking to the press, Owen looked like he could hardly wait. 'Driving in to training every morning, I think about what I'm doing for Liverpool and hopefully what I could do with England. It doesn't worry me at all, it doesn't scare me. I'm very excited, and my family are as thrilled as I am. As far as I'm concerned, I have the challenge of proving I'm good enough for the World Cup. I've got nothing to lose.'

*

A packed Wembley witnessed the birth of an England career but on the night it was Chile's Marcelo Salas who stole the headlines. Owen failed to continue his remarkable feat of scoring on his début at every level, but nevertheless proved to be at the heart of every good England move.

Sitting high up in the Wembley stands in the Olympic gallery, I had a stunning view of the length and breadth of the pitch and could really appreciate for the first time Owen's frightening pace and the effect he had on defenders. It was clear they weren't sure whether to push up or sit back and allow him to attack.

Despite the fact that England lost, Owen won the Man of the Match award and Hoddle was delighted with his performance. 'It was the best international début by an eighteen-year-old I have seen. It certainly hasn't hindered his chances of going to the World Cup.'

The 2–0 defeat had brought England back down to earth after the euphoria of qualifying in Rome; Hoddle thought this was no bad thing. 'You're never happy being beaten, but it's not a disaster. I was never going to lose in the long term. You can't lose when you're experimenting. It just shows you that this World Cup is not going to be a stroll. We can obviously put on a more experienced side. But I felt, right from the first whistle, that we just weren't on our toes. The two new lads up front [Owen and Dublin] did very well on their débuts. Very well indeed.'

'It wasn't a good team performance, but I felt I did all right,' Owen said after the game. 'I could have been a lot better, but I could also have been a lot worse. I'm quite pleased. I had one chance early on which came to me quite quickly. I hit it with the outside of my foot, but maybe I should have given it some power instead of trying to place the ball. The South Americans showed that they are very good on the ball and can cause big problems, and that's what they did to us tonight.

'The fact that I was creating a new record didn't affect me during the game. In the build-up I was told early that I would be playing by Glenn Hoddle and it was a great feeling.'

Shearer approved of Owen's début performance and was fulsome in his praise for the boy in the post-match press conference.

'There were no nerves beforehand. There wasn't anything. The way he went about things, you'd think he'd been around for a long, long time. He wasn't frightened at all. Michael was one of the positive things to come out of the game. Let's put it this way – he hasn't done his World Cup chances any harm, has he? He's certainly given Glenn Hoddle something to think about.'

Owen had had a wonderful night. A packed Wembley saw the launch of a new star and, as we drifted away in the cool evening air, the possibility that in six months' time France would be seeing the eighteen-year-old light up the World Cup was beginning to gel in people's heads. You could pinch yourself for thinking it, but England might, just might, have another World Cup star on their hands . . .

CHAPTER FOUR

England expects

Monsieur Guilland lived on the outskirts of the forest of Escoublac, a gathering of pine trees that form a vast green shield around the resort of La Baule.

I'd driven to the west coast from Paris, losing my way briefly in a violent storm outside Nantes. I had to fight my way through the horrendous rain to catch sight of road signs that even the locals would tell you were of little value if you sought the right directions. And this was the start of summer.

I finally collected the keys to the house a couple of hours later at the travel agency in a place called Pinochet, a retirement area for posh Parisians. A bit like Bournemouth, only more attractive.

Ford had kindly donated something called a 'people carrier' for the trip – a purple contraption that guzzled fuel but ate up the road. It could seat up to nine souls but I never had more than a couple at a time in the back of mine. I parked the car opposite Monsieur Guilland's house and wandered up to my villa: base camp for the next five weeks, if England lasted that long.

Nothing worked. The heating instructions, not surprisingly, were in French but, worse, I had to struggle to locate the gas and water terminals around the house before making further progress. I had one neighbour looking in the front garden, worming his way down drainpipes and scooting round the back for God-knows-what before I could offload half my bags from the back of the car.

The neighbour's wife seemed to be oblivious to the fact that I couldn't understand a word of what she was saying and it was only on the arrival of the friendly M. Guilland that some sense of order was restored.

M. Guilland was a businessman who travelled extensively in England, and as a result he spoke perfect English. His two daughters went to the school whose training pitch England had commandeered for the next month. The girls were more upset that David Beckham had turned up without his Spice Girl on his arm. And I thought the French had taste.

I was furnished with this information that evening as M. Guilland and I sat down at his place for a few beers in front of Cameroon *v* Austria. (My heating had been fixed but the fixtures and fittings were designed in the 1970s by a hippy who probably listened to too much Gong; the one-star accommodation promised in the travel brochure was one star too many.) There was a charming moment when the two daughters, aged six and eight, stood to attention at the foot of the stairs before being beckoned over to us. They curtseyed and said '*bonjour*' before scurrying off up to their rooms. Polite without going overboard about it.

French TV has a habit of accentuating the positive in anything it deems worth while. From the Coca-Cola adverts full of kids prancing gaily round the fields of France – to the tune of Blondie's 'Atomic' – to the screaming commentators demanding our '*Att-en-ti-on! Att-en-ti-on!*' every time a player got the ball into the penalty box, the telly was doing its bit to get the French public excited.

Unlike Hansen and O'Neill, when French TV pundits argued amongst themselves, the scatter-gun delivery of their language and the fact that there would usually be six or seven of them on the panel meant the TV camera had to swing from left to right as if it were recording an episode of *This Life*. The pair of resident hosts would grin inanely but their fake tan seemed to melt under the studio lights as the tournament progressed. Pouting Beatrice Dalle lookalikes were dragged on to chat about the best-looking players in the World Cup and the audience were encouraged to wear their nation's shirts, *Fantasy Football*-style. One joker, not dissimilar in appearance to the bald professor from TV's *The Great Egg Race*, had a theory he was happy to share with us: it was England's turn to win the World Cup because, since 1966, the winners had won the tournament in the following order: Brazil 1970, Germany 1974, Argentina 1978, Italy 1982, Argentina 1986, Germany 1990 and Brazil 1994. The theory didn't do much for Monsieur Guilland. His money was on the French. And he was an Arsenal fan, too.

★

Tony Adams was having a quiet World Cup. He'd had his AA councillor pop over to France but far from this being an emergency call, Adams was sounding happier than ever.

Philosophical and keen to tackle anything in front of him, he'd been reading a couple of books on tour: Christopher Reeves's autobiography *Still Me* (a reflection of life since the catastrophic riding accident that paralysed the former *Superman* star); and a book entitled *The Diving Bell and the Butterfly* written by former *Elle* magazine editor Jean-Dominique Bauby. (Bauby had suffered a massive stroke a few years ago and was left speechless and paralysed apart from one muscle in his eyelid. In spite of this, he was still able to write a 130-page book; from a signal via his eyelid he dictated one letter at a time – 200,000 blinks in all!)

It was inspirational stuff, and the Arsenal captain was happy to talk to anyone about it. He was enjoying the chance to show the world what he could do. There were even rumblings in the press that he was England's answer to Italy's legendary captain, Franco Baresi.

It was a far cry from the mountain of criticism that used to feature so regularly in newspaper articles about England's 'dodgy back-four – good in the air, but slow on the ground'.

'It wasn't reality a lot of the time,' says Adams, lying back in the sun.

The rain had finally left La Baule and we were being treated to what promised to be the start of some decent weather. Mind you, it didn't bother Adams if it rained or shined. For a man who famously takes every day as it comes, he was just grateful to be here. 'I'm not saying it's totally black and white. I'm not saying all I could do was head a ball and tackle and now I go forward and it's beautiful and I score wonderful goals. If you look back, that player could play a bit as well.

'Okay, I might have been suffering but I was winning things that way. My opinion then was "I'm young, I have four trophies at twenty-two. How dare you say I shouldn't be playing this way?" I've changed. Arsène Wenger has been wonderful in the past two years. He's not said, "Go forward, go inside-right." I still defend. I think I'm a pretty good defender. I play to my strengths. It would be foolish of me to try to play like Dennis Bergkamp.

'I'm not going to float upfield and sacrifice what I'm good at for the team. There is this imaginary media figure of a fantastic footballer who gets the ball, takes four forwards on and runs upfield.'

Asked if he thought the rule changes and FIFA's insistence that referees came down hard on bad tackles made his job more difficult, Adams was philosophical. 'Good players can adapt. It's the same situation as a few years ago when the press were saying it was all over for the Arsenal defence now that there was no tackle from behind and you can't pass back to the goalkeeper. We've proved that good players can adapt. We've won another league title.'

The reminiscence was short. 'The Double is history. It's a lovely memory and I get a little shiver now and again. The important thing for Tony Adams is to look forward and get on with the next challenge. I live day by day. I'm having a pretty good day today. I've just read a book.

'Who said I was on a high when we won the Double? I had a good day at the office. That's where I get my self-esteem. I'm a realist. I could have a depressing, horrible day. My philosophy is just trying to get better next day.

'I'm true to myself today. I've lightened up a lot. I've got rid of all the guilt and the shame. I don't worry about journalists because I know they've got nothing on me. I haven't any ghosts in the cupboard any more. There's a lot of freedom to what I actually do today. And then I can smile and lead my life happy and contented.'

Paul Gascoigne was sitting on a beach in Florida at this moment, as far removed from the way Adams was feeling as you can get. 'Paul's a wonderful, happy, lovely soul. But I'm not Paul. I'm Tony Adams. All I said to Paul is that I'm here. There is an element of sadness. I want a fit, talented Paul Gascoigne playing at this World Cup. It's not to be. We've got to move on. Every time you ask "Should Paul be playing?" it's like talking about whether George Best was the best player in the world in 1970. Talking about other individuals does a disservice to the twenty-two trying to win the World Cup for England.'

Adams was looking forward to the game against Tunisia and was impressed with what he'd seen so far. But he wasn't in awe of any player.

'I've got to look at the foreign strikers but I don't hype them like the press do,' he said. 'I keep it in reality: right foot, left foot, good in the air, strengths, weaknesses, quick, strong. That's my job. I'll watch videos of them. We've been doing it for years. Sometimes the media forget we can be so professional.

'I was seventeen and talking to Pat Rice, who used to keep a notebook on left-wingers. I wanted to learn. I said, "That's a really good idea, Pat." He said, "Look at all this, this left-winger comes inside, this one's quick."

'I went home and put Cyril Regis on my computer and then

Garry Thompson. Some players are obvious. I know Dennis Berg-kamp inside out.'

And if England did well, he might be playing against him later in the tournament.

*

England were developing a habit for playing matches behind closed doors. First Caen and now this; their best XI against the rest. Rumour had it that young Beckham was in the reserves. Darren Anderton was on the right-wing. Old Sicknote himself. You couldn't find a journalist in the country who thought that was a good idea. Beckham had played in all eight of England's World Cup qualifiers and Anderton had barely dragged himself off the physio's table to play a handful of Tottenham's matches. You couldn't believe he was match-fit.

So it was with heavy heart and a certain amount of trepidation that I drove up to the Golf de La Baule golf club on that Friday morning, just north of the resort, hidden away in the woods around Escoublac. Gendarmes guarded the entrance to the club and on the way up I was pulled over by three of them. The sight of armed policemen is always a shocker. It was hard to take your eyes off the bulging holsters strapped to the side of the coppers' waists. My trusty accreditation dangling from my neck, however, I was waved along.

I parked the car and noticed the proliferation of British number plates in the carpark. La Baule isn't that far from the ferry port of St Malo if you fancied a drive. I strolled up to the first tee and passed David Seaman and Martin Keown. They were on their way to the clubhouse and were dressed in their regulation Umbro polo shirts. I congratulated them on the Arsenal Double. 'Cheers,' said Seaman. Laughing, jovial, everything you'd expect. Seaman had become a man of the people ever since he received a standing ovation at Wimbledon after his heroics at Euro '96. Keown appeared to have other things on his mind and, as Tony Adams had already mentioned, the Double seemed a long time ago now they were in France.

The snappers were busy as Teddy Sheringham and Alan Shearer swung what looked like three-irons on the edge of the first tee. They were both rather dapper in their omnipresent polo shirts and brogues. The photographers were three-deep on the right-hand side as you looked at the green, chatting eagerly, old hands cracking jokes with England's back-room staff. So Teddy was teeing off with Shearer. Was this a hint that the Manchester United forward had got the nod from Hod?

Alan Shearer grinned like a fat Cheshire cat. *He* was playing, no doubt about that. I'd watched Shearer throughout the two years England had been qualifying for this World Cup and in that time he'd changed from an obdurate, monosyllabic interviewee to the jovial, knowing *charmer* that we had in front of us now. Henry Winter from the *Daily Telegraph* put it down to the contentious tackle on Neil Lennon at the end of the season. 'Ever since then he's realised his nice-guy image was slipping. He's decided to muck in and become one of the lads,' said Winter.

★

'We really have to win our first match against Tunisia in Marseille to energise the team as a whole. That's why, for the second training-session, I put the players in a match situation. For four or five years now, England has progressed enormously – both technically and tactically. Players like Alan Shearer and Michael Owen have unquestionably been a plus in our training. But I don't want to play them together because they don't operate the same way. I'm obviously very happy to kick off in Marseille, a city that's as passionate about football as the big English cities are.'

So read a statement from Glenn Hoddle.

'What does Owen have to do to get in the team?' demanded one hack.

'He should go off for a weekend on the piss,' answered another.

Kevin Keegan was staying in Bordeaux for ITV's World Cup coverage. He had no doubts about Owen. 'I know what I would do, but then I'm not the manager. I think he gives us something different. Sheringham and Shearer proved themselves in Euro '96, but that was two years ago. Owen is young, he's quick, he's brave. And despite what Glenn Hoddle says about him not being a natural goalscorer, if he's not, I don't know who is! He has been scoring goals ever since he was born, it seems. I would like him to stay in the side. He will certainly have a part to play in this World Cup, I am sure of that.'

*

Back on the golf course Michael Owen and Paul Scholes were the next pair to tee-off. They were playing a four-ball with Shearer and Sheringham. Owen had come on and scored in his second England showing against Morocco and the tabloids were whipping up a campaign to get him in the starting line-up. His golf was as solid as his football and both he and Scholes joined the SAS boys on the green with one shot.

Paul Merson was a surprise call-up for the final twenty-two but his golf wasn't up to much. His golf shot veered off to the left while Rob Lee, David Batty and David Seaman hit the green. It was a credit to the man that he was here at all after all his problems and he looked fit and raring to go. He was also the only person in the squad playing First Division football.

While Gazza was resting his belly on a bar in Florida, Merson and Adams, two men who had the courage to face their demons in public and battle to overcome various addictions, were here in France. Whatever you said about Hoddle, he stood by his men if they stood by him. It was sending out a message to the rest of the world about our battling boozers. The players that is, not the fans.

Hoddle and John Gorman were sitting in their golf buggy. Photographers swarmed around them, jostling for position, and such was the commotion, they nearly turned the cart over. The England manager snapped. 'Give us a minute here, lads!' he said.

The press weren't happy either. There was a man from Scotland Yard patrolling the grass and he wasn't having any nonsense. Rather brusquely, he instructed us as to what we could or could not get up to. 'Mind the grass', 'keep off the lawn', that sort of thing. A bit like an obtrusive tour guide on one of those dreadful 18-30 package trips.

'I don't mean to be a pain,' said a senior lensman to the FA's press officer, Steve Double, 'but this wanker's stopping us from doing our job!'

The press-liaison man was having a tough job keeping the boys happy. A couple of players were trotted out to see us each day but you could feel that the resentment towards the England set-up, and towards Hoddle in particular, was growing.

*

David Beckham admitted that it would be 'the most disappointing moment of my entire career' if he was left out of England's starting line-up against Tunisia in Marseille. The idea that the Manchester United pin-up would miss out had never entered anyone's head, in particular his. But here we were, four days before kick-off, and Beckham was feeling sidelined. Was he really going to be dropped?

Surely with Gazza out, Beckham and Anderton might play in the same team? But then Hoddle would have to break up the Ince/Batty axis. And that wasn't likely.

'If I am not in the starting line-up I will be totally gutted. Everything has gone so well for me so far that to experience something like that would be extremely hard to take. I desperately want to play. I desperately want to be out there. I desperately want to play a role for England in the World Cup,' he told a waiting group of writers.

Hoddle had faith in Beckham's right foot and had declared him the best crosser of the ball in the Premiership. If there was any criticism of Beckham at all, it was that he could give the ball away at times. With Anderton nearly fit, Hoddle had at last given himself an option on the right.

Beckham commented: 'Darren has come from nowhere. But all I can do is carry on playing my normal game. I cannot afford to worry about anything else or anyone else who is playing well.

'You are constantly looking over your shoulder and just trying not to think about [being dropped]. But it is a very strange situation for me to be in. In the past it has always been me trying to get in front of someone else, so the situation has been reversed. I'm the one out there to be shot at,' he finished.

Later I asked Graeme Le Saux what he thought about it. 'There's been some pretty debatable journalism over the last few weeks,' he said, referring to the question-marks over Anderton's fitness.

★

That afternoon I saw the Paraguay goalkeeper Chilavert hit an excellent free-kick narrowly over the crossbar in an otherwise dull draw with Bulgaria. The Danes didn't look good either, beating Saudi Arabia 1–0, and we waited expectantly for the final game in Group C, France against South Africa.

I dined with Tom Jenkins and *The Guardian*'s chief football writer David Lacey. They were staying in a villa away from the main press camp who were bedded down at the four-star L'Hermitage hotel. Lacey expressed his satisfaction that Hoddle had dumped 'the idiotic Gascoigne'. At least now the press wouldn't waste time chasing him for stories every day, he said. You got the feeling he wasn't Gazza's greatest fan.

We discussed the World Cup and Lacey talked at length about the squad system the favourites were using. 'It's thirty-two countries now and Brazil's Mario Zagallo has already said he can't win the World Cup with eleven men.' This explained why Leonardo of AC Milan and Denilson, soon to become the world's most expensive player in a £21 million move to Real Betis in Spain, had started on the bench against Scotland.

France kicked off with the likes of Pirès, Trézéguet, Vieira and Djorkaeff on the bench and David Ginola in the stands for the BBC. When Barry Davies commented on *Match of the Day* that Aimé Jacquet must have a hell of a team to leave out Ginola, he was right. You only had to look at the bench to figure that one out.

We discussed the difference between France '98 and Lacey's experience of USA '94 and Italia '90. The Italians were mad, passionate and besotted with the game, and the people in the States were bonkers as well, but in the sense that they wanted to show enthusiasm for the sport. It was a reflection of the national characteristic and stereotype.

The French, in contrast, took things as they came. They were proud to be hosting the tournament but weren't about to let it become the centre of attention. The national side walloped South Africa 3–0, with Christophe Dugarry coming on as a substitute to groans of derision and then scoring – which got an even louder groan. According to one taxi-driver I spoke to in Nantes, the level of Dugarry's play depended on how much money you gave him to run. He didn't look too bad to me but his World Cup would come to something of a grinding, hamstring-pulling halt in the next match. France's star of the South Africa match was Thierry Henry, who scored his country's third. They would be a hard team to beat, but Lacey fancied Italy *v* Argentina for the final. We would see.

CHAPTER FIVE

The boy Beckham

David Robert Joseph Beckham was born in Leytonstone, east London, on 2 May 1975. The son of a kitchen-equipment maintenance man and a hairdresser, he was the second of three children who grew up in the Chingford area of the capital. As a junior schoolboy he played for the side the year above his own, and for a local club side, Ridgeway Rovers, where his potential was first spotted (he scored 101 goals in 115 games). At eleven he won a soccer skills tournament organised by Bobby Charlton, whose advice to him ever since has been to 'shoot at all times if you've got a chance'. Then came his first trip to Manchester United's summer school, and anxiety that a skinny kid, rejected by the England Schoolboys for his lack of height, could ever make it. 'I never thought of nothing else – I used to tell everyone and they'd laugh and say, "Yeah, but what else you gonna do?", and I'd say, "No, football." United was the dream.'

He was, he says, always a Manchester United supporter, drawn to the club by his father Ted's total devotion to all things red. They still joke in the Beckham household about who was the most excited when young David actually signed to United.

And yet, it was nearly all so different.

In January 1986 a scout came to watch Ridgeway Rovers and recommended Beckham to Tottenham Hotspur. The club had a fine tradition for spotting young talent and he was invited to train twice a week with the youth team and reserves at White Hart Lane.

'Even then I would turn up in my red Man United kit. I got a lot of stick for that,' he recalls with a smile on his face.

The influence of his dad's love for Man United still prevailed but it was an intervention by the United player whom Beckham would later be compared to, Sir Bobby Charlton, that finally took the teenager up north. He left Chingford High at sixteen, having failed his small crop of GCSEs, and travelled north to join United's training scheme, living in lodgings and seeing his parents at weekends. It was a drastic change of scene but one that proved helpful in unexpected ways. Not being able to hang out with all his old school-mates meant it wasn't so easy to be dragged into going out at night into pubs and clubs, stuff that would detract from his burgeoning career as a full-time footballer.

At Old Trafford, the club was so big and the stars that played for it so great, there was no chance of slacking, thinking you knew it all. There he was surrounded by other lads just as talented, just as desperate for a chance to prove themselves. For the first time in his life, Beckham was learning to fight for his place in the team.

'At United, the kids are hungry for success – that's just how it is,' says defender and club stalwart Gary Pallister. 'Here you're not just playing against other teams but against people coming through at the club. You have to earn your place, otherwise you're out of the team. And once you've been at Old Trafford, there's only one place you're going and that's down.'

It's the kind of pressure that keeps you humble and focused. As an apprentice, Beckham would be one of the first at the training-ground every morning, cleaning boots and sweeping floors – anything to get noticed by the manager, Alex Ferguson. You can't imagine George Best doing that.

United had just won the European Cup-Winners' Cup when Beckham joined the club, but had not won the league title for twenty-three years. Nevertheless, they were fondly regarded as the most glamorous side in English football. Certainly they were one of the biggest. Young internationals and old trophies fill Old Trafford and becoming part of that great tradition can be an intimidating experience for a fresh-faced lad from London.

'When you first arrive at Manchester United, you're scared of just about everything,' says Beckham's room-mate and good friend Gary Neville, who was signed at the same time as Beckham.

'It is a dream to play here,' says Gary's brother, Philip. 'Walking out of the tunnel is amazing. At about 2.55 p.m. on a Saturday, to hear the roar from those 58,000 people, it's the biggest noise I've ever heard.'

Beckham's move up the ladder from trainee to first-teamer was fast. At the start of the 1996–97 season, a goal struck from inside his own half against Wimbledon secured the player a place in football folklore. John Motson described the goal on *Match of the Day* as 'Absolutely phenomenal! David Beckham – surely an England player for the future – scores a goal that will be talked about and replayed for years!' It had only been three years since he'd been out on loan to Preston North End, but that goal and a couple of notable strikes from outside the penalty-box ensured a call-up for Glenn Hoddle's first England World Cup qualifier against Moldova. Beckham hasn't looked back since.

★

By turns the most admired and the most reviled player in England, David Beckham has developed from that first match in Moldova to the playmaker he is today. Post-Gazza, Beckham has become the nearest thing we have to someone who can lay on a killer pass, even if he lacks the Geordie's ability to dribble past the opposition. Touching the sun? A genius, perhaps?

'Even from youth level, I've always scored goals that were, er, spectacular,' said Beckham, waiting patiently for the call to arms for the Tunisia match.

It was the weekend before the trip to Marseille and Beckham seemed relaxed, looking good in training.

'I've never really been a tap-in type of player,' he went on. 'The goals I have scored have created an expectation, but I've put myself in there and I've got to live up to it.'

Behind the wheel of his Porsche 911, Beckham exudes all the class and confidence the ownership of such a design classic can bring. Man and machine in harmony. When he peels off his track-suit to reveal a body sculpted purely for the purpose of playing ball, men look on in awe and ladies lust like the mob in that drinks commercial. (It's so good I can't remember what the ad is for!) Legs far chunkier than the thighs of a pedigree racehorse, torso stripped of any excess fat, a footballer's body is like that of a boxer's turned on its head, with all the muscle below the belt. Beckham runs his hand through the well-cut hair now a lot blonder (was that the sun or the bottle?), carefully flicking the strands that fall asymmetrically over the corner of each eyebrow. Striking a model's pose, smiling shyly at the wonder of it all, David Beckham understands. His time has come.

It is this image, this portrayal of arrogance, that incenses some supporters. Few have had to endure the abuse that Beckham gets every Saturday during the season; the references to Posh Spice and variations on a sexual position.

'Yes, I can hear it, and yes, it gets to me,' he admits. 'It's not very nice hearing things about my private life like that, I don't think anyone would like it. But as a professional footballer you can't be worried about fans giving you stick. No matter how bad it gets, you can't afford to let if affect your game. The best way to cope with it is to stick one in the top corner. I used to think that was the perfect response, but if it is not possible, it is still important to keep playing and just black out the abuse. I've learned how to do that. Stuff I hear from the terraces will never affect me in games. Because at the end of the day, they are up there watching, aren't they? I'm the one playing, they have paid to come in.'

The calmer, more mature Beckham cited *Le Tournoi* last year as a turning point for himself. An outburst of petulance against France cost him the chance to play Brazil when he argued with the referee and, since then, Hoddle had told him to stop losing his temper and cut down on the number of unnecessary yellow cards he was picking up. 'It doesn't seem like a year ago,' he said. 'It seems like it was only yesterday, because everyone keeps mentioning it.'

Beckham's club form dipped a little towards the end of the season. Alex Ferguson had consistently said that the youngsters might not last an entire season. It was a measure of the success that United had achieved with their kids that we thought of them as veterans.

Did Beckham feel he'd lost an edge, had he calmed down to the detriment of other areas of his game?

'I might not have scored many spectacular goals this season but I think I have been contributing. I've played in every game for United and every game for England, so my form can't be that disappointing, can it?

'I feel as if I've done quite well for England so far but I'd like to do better; I definitely think there's better to come. I've still got a lot to learn at this level, and I'm still putting in a lot of practice on the training-pitch. I don't tell myself I'm brilliant at this or that and don't need to do any more work on it. [Beckham once told me he practised taking up to fifty free-kicks every day, after the rest of the United lads had finished for the session.] But I can't deny that a few goals would be nice. Scoring a goal for your country must be one of the best things you can do as a footballer. I nearly got one in Rome, and I had a chance against Portugal, but there's no point dwelling on missed opportunities. It will happen when it happens.'

Like everything in his life, Beckham was sure he'd score. He seemed equally confident that he'd start the match against Tunisia, possibly in his favoured central midfield role.

'I played against Italy in *Le Tournoi* in a semi-central role with Paul Ince and Paul Scholes, and I thought I had one of my most effective games for England. I felt comfortable there, and I do prefer playing in the middle, but it's up to the manager. He's got other players who can play in the middle, and I don't mind playing on the right. Being in the team is still the most important thing for me, both for United and for England.

'If the choice was mine I'd say middle, but it is probably significant that both Alex Ferguson and Glenn Hoddle have mentioned my crossing ability from the right this season. I don't feel I can argue. I've even got the No 7 at United now, instead of my old No 10, which I was a bit disappointed to have to give up. I know the No 7 is a very famous shirt at Old Trafford, and some great players have worn it, but I was quite happy with the continental idea that 10 is the special number. But the simple fact is I've only played one game in the centre for United this season, against Barnsley. Even at home I'm in the team as a right-winger.'

It was strange, in retrospect, to sit there listening to Beckham talk about shirt numbers. The very idea that he might not play at all hadn't even been considered. It was a formality, a toss-up. Centre of midfield or right wing.

He joked with me once that he'd go in goal for England, but this was serious. This was the World Cup, the chance to compare yourself with the best in the world. In the modern, money-driven game it wasn't just about playing for your country. It was about making a name for yourself. Cashing in. Becoming a superstar.

But it wasn't arrogance nor even the naïvety of youth. It was what every hungry pro needs. *Belief.* And Beckham had bucketfuls of it. Hoddle clearly had other ideas.

Mind you, you couldn't blame Beckham for thinking his time had come. With Gascoigne out, the door was open for a new playmaker. And, if it was a choice between him and Steve McManaman, well . . .

'I watched every game in Italia '90 at my mum and dad's in London. I dreamed of doing the same thing. Gazza was my hero, just like he was everyone else's. Everything about him, everything that went with Gazza in that World Cup, was so exciting. He was brilliant. The World Cup is massive, and though I've played in some big games for Manchester United, nothing compares to this feeling of going out to face the world. I'd love to make the same sort of impact as Gazza did in 1990. You might even see me cry; I am a very emotional person too, but at the moment I've no plans for that.'

Author's note: So let's get something straight right here. No matter how much footballers earn and the fact that they make a living out of knocking a ball around a field twice a week, who'd trade places with the bloke who just made that statement, given what we know happened next? Hmm . . . thought not.

*

Beckham, like Tony Adams, was sorry that Gazza couldn't be in France. You wondered who were the senior players who had asked Hoddle to sort out Gazza and his booze problem.

'You sort of fall in love with Paul Gascoigne when you play in the same squad. He's such a wonderful person to have around,' said Beckham. 'I'm sorry he's not with us, but we have still got a squad of great players here, and not only that but a real club atmosphere.

'That is something Glenn Hoddle's squads have been strong on from the start. We are a tight unit but one capable of having a laugh and a joke. Just like you get at a club. Some people get up your nose, but there are always others to help you see the funny side. With the players we have, and the way we get along together, I think England can achieve a really high level in this World Cup.'

With that, Beckham was off. He didn't want to talk about the previous day's training match which had seen Anderton in his position on the flanks and he wasn't keen to comment on the wearing of a sarong snapped while he was away on holiday with his fiancée Victoria Adams. He'd said his piece and had said it frankly and to the point. There were few scraps for the press boys to feed on, but one thing was for sure: England were running a slick publicity operation here in La Baule.

★

Glenn Hoddle answered a barrage of questions on the eve of the Tunisia match. Asked how he'd assessed the team's performances after their training, he replied: 'England will be ready for its début in the World Cup on Monday. It's fair to say that I believe there has never been an England team better prepared for a World Cup. [Staying in La Baule] was successful for us last year. After the disappointment for everyone in England of not being in the US in 1994, we are thrilled to be part of France '98.'

Hoddle had little reason to enjoy these moments. He had been treated poorly by the press as a player – no doubt smarting from the 'Glenda' tag the tabloids attached to him – and he rarely felt the desire to explain his thoughts or motivations to people who hadn't played the game themselves. Asked how far the team's ambitions went, he replied: 'Every one of our twenty-two players has a role to play. I believe they are relaxed and confident about the task in front of all of us. There is nothing bigger in the life of a footballer than playing in the World Cup finals. We believe we are in one of the strongest and toughest groups of all. After all, three of the four teams are in the top twelve of the FIFA rankings. Anyway, there are no easy games in international football any more. We believe that any one of six or seven teams could win the World Cup. We're one of them. There's no question it will be a very tight tournament and the dividing line between success and failure will be very thin.'

Hoddle's capacity to talk in clichés and religious mumbo-jumbo was astounding the press boys. His constant use of words like 'belief' and 'destiny' put him up there with Obi-Wan Kenobi and his old pal Uri Geller. If I had a pound for every time I've heard a manager say 'There are no easy games in international football'. . .

★

Darren Anderton was doing his best to ignore the mounting campaign for David Beckham to maintain his spot on the right wing. It was ironic that at one time, two years ago, Manchester United almost bought him to fill the position Beckham later made his own at Old Trafford. After four hernias and one groin operation Anderton was seeking to make up for lost time but he knew his role as an out-and-out winger would need to be tempered with some stout defending.

One criticism that had been levelled at Beckham was that he didn't tackle back – though many of his supporters believed this was unfounded. Beckham was surely the best crosser of the ball in the squad and, with Alan Shearer on fire, England needed crosses.

Anderton, though, was having none of it: 'Marking and tackling is not my game but whenever I've played wide I've never had a problem with it – although patrolling up and down the flank can be tiring and demanding.

'I spent the early part of my career as an orthodox winger and could attack the box knowing I always had a full-back behind me. Now I know I am expected to do much more work covering back but I'm confident there will be no problems.

'I accept criticism made about my defending in the wing-back position but I would like to remind people that three years ago I played against Roberto Carlos. He's probably the best player in the world in his position at the moment, but I had no problems against him that day. I rather liked it.' (England lost 3–1 to Brazil that day, with Juninho, Ronaldo and the madman Edmundo scoring for Brazil. Le Saux grabbed England's only goal. Terry Venables admitted that he'd wanted Anderton to track back but also make sure Roberto Carlos was forced 'to follow Darren up the field'. Anderton would be all right in the role.)

The Tottenham winger was asked about Beckham. Was there any rivalry?

'I almost went to Manchester United before he became famous and had made his name but since then he has become a wonderful player and I wish him the greatest of luck. He has always played the wing-forward role for England although he likes the central midfield position. It's the same with me. I enjoy playing down the side but would rather play in the middle. However, that doesn't matter. This is England and the World Cup and you would play anywhere.'

Anderton was desperate to make up for what he called 'two lost years' after doing well in Euro '96. 'It would have been nice for me to go on and do well with England after Euro '96 but since then it's been a disaster for me. However, now I'm at the World Cup and the realisation has finally hit that I am back. It's only just beginning to dawn on me that I'm about to have a dream come true. It feels great. For two years I thought I was going to miss the World Cup but now all that can be forgotten.

'We've been watching the World Cup on television and the play has been tremendous. I have also watched previous ones on the box. Now I have the chance to play in one and I can't wait for England to get going.'

Anderton left us to mull on that point and went off to rejoin his friends at the team hotel. While journalists sifted through the notes from his discussion one thing was clear. Anderton knew he was in the team for Tunisia. But what about Beckham?

CHAPTER SIX

Port of storm

For five and a half days an Englishman abroad had little concern for matters other than the composition of his nation's seam attack and the faint suspicion that Parisian waiters might have seen him coming.

France '98 began with the cacophony of samba and bagpipes and there was every indication that the exuberance of Nigeria and Cameroon was more than a one-off. The party had got off to a thrilling start. Now it was England's turn.

I had a few hours to kill in Nantes before boarding my train. A friendly policeman gave me directions for the Copacabana beach; the local authorities had imported thousands of tons of sand to recreate Rio's famous beach volleyball pitches and they were holding a wonderful competition in the town's main square.

In the foreground of the town's Cathédrale de St-Pierre-et-St-Paul I watched kids play beach football. Lovers walked hand in hand round the sandy arena. Nigerian fans who had just seen the most thrilling game in the World Cup so far commiserated with Spanish supporters still stunned by their team's defeat. Pelé was on TV. France '98 was shaping up nicely.

I arrived in Marseille after spending eleven hours on a steam train from Nantes that will live long in the memory as something of an old boiler. It was an overnight trip and I was holed up in a *couchette*, a form of on-board lodging comprising two three-tier bunk-beds stuffed into a room no bigger than is strictly necessary.

As the train made its way south through Brittany to Bordeaux and on to the Mediterranean, it was pleasant to lie for a while in the tiny cabin smoking a cigarette and to feel alone in the darkness, away from it all.

The rhythmical sound as the wheels rattled over the points was an agreeable background to the pattern of my thoughts and to canter through the French heartland made one feel like an old-fashioned adventurer. And at the end of the journey was the unknown.

Marseille was lit up by a bright sun on the Sunday morning as our train pulled in to the Gare de St Charles. I took a deep breath of satisfaction as I stretched my legs on disembarking and considered the possibilities of a croissant and some coffee.

At 7.15 a.m. the only outlet for such fare was the station's McDonald's, and, although there is something deeply grating about entering the portals of the junk food empire in the world's culinary centre, I was tired and hungry and the coffee smelled fresh.

The first sight that greeted me was a group of England fans slobbered over a collection of tables and chairs to the right of the counter. You could tell they were English by the flags, sunburn and tattoos. All that was missing was beer, but there'd be plenty of that later. From their accents it was clear that they hailed from the West Country, and their passion for clubs like Torquay and Bristol City was written large on the omnipresent cross of St George.

The bemused attendant behind the counter smiled rather gamely at their efforts to order Big Macs and Coke in nothing but the broadest of English, and I was glad I was able to greet her and place my order in French.

It was much warmer here than on the west coast and I decided to relax beside the swimming-pool at my hotel. I was staying quite a long way from the centre of Marseille and the journey there by bus had been sweltering. I overheard the conversation of three Manchester United fans at the poolside who spoke of fights breaking out the previous night by the old port. Apparently a car had run over an English fan and hundreds of English supporters had steamed into the driver, causing a disturbance. Well, you can just imagine it.

Le Vieux-Port had been earmarked by our hosts as the place to hold festivals and concerts prior to England's match with Tunisia, just as the organisers had been doing in other cities throughout the country. But 'our boys' were making sure that, for this World Cup, England supporters would be attended by riot police bearing CS gas canisters and machine-guns rather than the culture and spectacle that was being served up elsewhere.

I sauntered down to the port on that Sunday afternoon to witness for myself how things were going. Coming out of one of Marseille's two Metro lines, a gangly Tunisian draped in a red flag enquired menacingly if I was 'Engleeesh'. He was wielding a long thin stick and had surrounded himself with a gaggle of mates. I told him I was American and got out of there sharpish.

At the port, I came across England supporters drinking heavily at the Blue Bar while members of the local gendarmerie slouched against a wall, smoking cigarettes and looking bored. Tunisians gathered in small numbers and chanted songs in the direction of the sunburnt minority.

I went off to another bar to watch Japan take on Argentina. A pleasant group of England lads were sitting around a table watching the game. They confirmed the story about fighting the night before. They'd left the Old Port and gone in search of some culture to the north of the port in Le Panier, the oldest part of Marseille where, up until the last war, tiny streets, steep steps and houses of every era formed a *vieille ville* typical of the Côte d'Azur. In 1943, however, with Marseille under German occupation, the quarter became an unofficial ghetto for *Untermensche* of every sort, including Resistance fighters, Communists and Jews. The Nazis gave the twenty thousand inhabitants one day's notice to quit. Many were deported to the camps. Dynamite was carefully laid, and everything was blown sky-high. The Germans had left three old buildings intact. After a couple of days in Marseille, you could sympathise with those wartime refugees.

The Japanese played gamely and if they'd had a decent striker might have put one over the South Americans. The winners of this group would play the runners-up in England's. There didn't seem much to worry Adams and co here.

★

Leaving the bar after the match, I noticed the whistles and jeers the moment I hit the pavement. Tunisians had gathered in far greater numbers and were driving round and round the one-way system rather like cowboy-chasing Indians chastising their dim-witted sunhat-wearing foe. It was hard to tell who were the good guys and who were the bad.

The atmosphere had changed from jovial badgering to something more sinister. I overheard quite a few English voices saying 'Why should we put up with this?' and 'This isn't on' as, by now, the bars were shut and even McDonald's had a bouncer guarding the toilets.

I stood outside the Old Port's Metro, the same spot at which I'd earlier encountered the inquisitive Tunisian. Now, though, the area was taken over by English fans. Everyone was drunk. I stopped off at the busy McDonald's and shoved my way past the slavering idiots unable to order even a coffee – 'What do you mean, you don't speak English, you fucking wanker?' When a number of them overheard me ordering my food in French, I was surrounded by a chorus of 'Here, I'll have one of them as well, *encore*, mate, *encore!*' I was glad to get out of there.

Back at my vantage-point by the Metro, clutching my Maccy D burgers, I realised the rowdy Tunisians had moved right up in front of the English fans. They threw beer at the Tunisians and then one of them grabbed a red flag and set fire to it. A few bottles were lobbed by faceless characters from behind the front lines and, seemingly within seconds, Tunisians and English were engaging in what one newspaper would later describe as 'hand-to-hand combat'. Nice.

★

I made my way up to the Stade Vélodrome to take in the England training session. Glenn Hoddle had issued a statement that he was here to talk football. 'With the three-point rule, it's imperative to win. We'll have to be careful of Tunisia. They'll be very motivated by their return to the World Cup.

'These days there are no longer any "small" teams. The differences in performance levels are tending to be reduced. Take the example of the match between Argentina and Japan. We prepared for this match with a friendly against Morocco. The Moroccans and Tunisians have a similar style of play. We would be quite happy with a 1–0 victory.' Hoddle was doing well with his policy of talking lots but saying absolutely nothing.

Answering a question after the training session as to whether Alan Shearer was the best finisher in the world, Hoddle said that he wanted to set the record straight: 'I never said he was a better finisher; I said he was a better finisher for the England side.

'I think if Alan played for Brazil and Ronaldo played for England, they'd both find it a bit difficult, because their styles of play are completely different. Obviously Alan's style of play and his attributes are very good for English football and the England team, but Ronaldo, for me, is the best player in the world.'

Ronaldo and Shearer had both suffered injury worries leading up to the World Cup. The question was: would either of them break down?

★

More interesting than Hoddle's thoughts was this statement from the news service coming through to journalists written at 7.36 p.m. that evening . . .

'On the eve of the England *v* Tunisia match, which will take place on Monday, 15 June, at 2.30 p.m. in the Stade Vélodrome, the city of Marseille is turning white and red, the colours of the two countries' flags. Fans of the two teams are beginning to arrive in Marseille by air, land and sea.

'Fans coming from Tunisia have been mainly gathering in the Belsunce district where there is a large Tunisian community. As for the English, they are scattered throughout the city.

'For the Tunisian team, it is almost like playing at home as the number of Tunisian citizens living in Marseille, according to the consulate of Tunisia, is close to twenty thousand.

'On Sunday evening, the England team had a training session around 6 p.m., and nearly a thousand England fans, many of them wearing the shirt of their favourite football team, invaded the various bars which surround the stadium.

' "The troublemakers have stayed in England, we've come to party," said a small group of fans who sat round a table with their beers.

'The rivalries between different English clubs are set aside during the World Cup in order to support the national team, even though Liverpool supporters are not great fans of David Beckham who plays for their rival, Manchester United.

'Approximately twenty thousand English fans are expected on Monday, 15 June, in Marseille.'

Out there in the real world a TV crew was interviewing English fans as they waited outside the stadium entrance for a quick glimpse of their heroes. Steph and her husband were both Liverpool supporters who were here solely to see Michael Owen play. 'As long as I see him tomorrow I'll be happy,' said Steph.

The camera crews had been quick on the scene chiefly because they had been waiting all day for the English hooligans to kick-off.

The players went through their drills, sirens wailing in the streets. It was embarrassing to be English, to be seen to be associated with this. That evening I decided to hole up in the hotel but spotted scores of English people in reception preparing for a good night out. This would involve lobbing crash-barriers through shop windows and pouring beer down their necks before coming back to the hotel to blast out 'Three Lions' on the stereo at 4 a.m.

★

I didn't see any running battles over the next two days but I saw plenty of people running. I didn't see any fighting but I fought my way through an increasingly tense atmosphere and I have to assume that those sirens that blared out, morning to night, must have been attending something. Questions have been asked about the role of the police here, the actions of the large North African population in Marseille and the wisdom of playing this game on a Monday, thus giving the thugs two days' steady drinking before kick-off. While we're at it, many have questioned the sense in even allowing England to play in France at all.

Nobody knew what would happen in Toulouse, the venue for England's next match, and at the back of my mind was the spectre of a possible confrontation (for that is what it would be) with Germany in Lyon. What no one was addressing is quite why the English behave in this way – the lager-lout *Loaded* generation with nothing to offer but beer and brutality. Cruel Britannia.

The people who have come to watch these games are deeply unpleasant angry young men. Even if they don't cause trouble they look awful and they irritate one and all with their leering, swearing and boozing. The Scots aren't like this. They're here to fly their flag with pride, not shove it up the noses of those who greet them. England have come to Marseille to watch a game of football and left behind a trail of destruction and misery.

When I was a kid I used to come to the south of France on camping holidays with my brother, mum and dad. We always had to convince those old men who sit on the stoops of corner-shops, men who had engaged in real hand-to-hand combat, that my blond hair and blue eyes didn't mean I was German. Now it's the English that aren't welcome. Bald fat bastards singing 'If it weren't for us you'd be German,' while saluting their foe with fascist *Sieg Heils*. That's what those wankers did to the English name in Marseille. They should be locked up or flogged in public.

★

England walked out to a glorious roar at 2.30 p.m. on Monday, 15 June. This was their moment, the second-last match in the first round of games, and the Stade Vélodrome was packed – not, as had been predicted, with Tunisians, but with sunburnt lard-arses. And some football fans.

The cross of St George was draped from the top of the stadium which was three-quarters exposed to the bright blue sunlight. England fans were making the most noise heard so far in France '98 and you sensed the Tunisians were stunned. This was their town, or as good as, and these crazy English, these crazy drunken berks, were packed in. Thousands of them were singing 'Rule Britannia' and the dated 'No Surrender'; weren't we supposed to be patching things up with the IRA?

The stadium could seat sixty thousand and three-quarters of the ground was filled English fans; they'd been allocated just seven thousand tickets for the match, so the touts had obviously done a roaring trade (though not, as we later found out, as outlandish as elsewhere).

In order to buy a ticket for the Stade Vélodrome, local people, who had come to see France play South Africa the previous Thursday, had had to buy a book of tickets. It was these that were now being sold to the England supporters. So much for the proposed checking of tickets. A security officer told me later that their policy was only to check names on the tickets of people who 'looked like causing trouble'. It seemed a somewhat arbitrary system for spotting hooligans if you asked me.

It was weird seeing Adams, Shearer, Ince and Batty spreading the ball around. It had been eight years since an England team had graced the World Cup and it was easy to forget how important it all was. None of these boys had ever reached the finals before; Seaman had been in the squad for Italy but had been injured, and Adams had been unlucky to lose out to Mark Wright in Bobby Robson's final twenty-two. The question on everyone's lips, though, was where were Beckham and Owen?

Michael Owen, number 20 on the team sheet, received the loudest cheer when the players' names where read out over the stadium tannoy. Beckham had been replaced by Darren Anderton, so the midfield looked a tad lumpy with Ince and Batty controlling the middle. Paul Scholes was in the starting line-up but was playing more as a third forward with poor old Teddy. Steady Teddy, lost in no-man's land.

Scholes and Sheringham were effectively doing the same job, namely linking the play between the rest of the field and the final third. The trouble was, Shearer didn't look a hundred per cent match-fit and we knew Anderton was still feeling his way.

England may have been ponderous in their approach but Tunisia were dreadful. Scholes missed two sitters before Shearer nodded in our first. I popped off to the toilets in the media centre downstairs just before half-time. Gary Lineker was standing at the next cubicle. 'All we need is a win,' he said, as you do at moments like that. 'But let's face it, Tunisia are crap!' We had a bet on the final score; 2-0 was my choice. Lineker couldn't see us getting a second.

Sol Campbell, for one, was having a storming match. Like Marcel Desailly, his strength in the penalty area was incredible. He'd tackle a man, turn the ball while holding the player off, and walk away towards the Tunisian goal with the opponent trailing in his wake. It was an awesome sight.

Adams had a shaky start but settled before too long, while Le Saux looked good going forward but seemed hesitant in defence. Hoddle was asking a lot of his wing-backs, expecting them to fill in a 3-5-2 formation when we had possession and then switch immediately to 5-3-2 as soon as we lost the ball. It was as if we had thirteen players on the pitch. Well, that was the idea.

Sheringham nearly caught out the Tunisian keeper with a first-time effort that was hooked from the edge of the box but, apart from that, he brought nothing to the party. Teddy had suffered a massive dip in form towards the end of the season but up till now played well for England. Here, though, he looked past it, even against this lot.

At half-time Lineker and Chris Waddle were doing their thing for the BBC just above us. We cut out a lump of cardboard and held up the customary 'Hello Mum' sign. My mate Dan was sitting next to me and he reckoned we should have written salutations to our local boozers. 'Have you noticed how all the fans' flags have the names of pubs written on them whereas before they used to say they were from Shrewsbury, Oldham or St Ives?' he asked. Was this of cultural significance? I couldn't imagine the BBC boys picking up on that one.

Dan's mobile rang. It was one of his mates telling him he'd just seen his head on the telly behind Lineker. 'Fame at last,' sighed Dan.

'More like notoriety,' I replied. 'It probably had a caption reading: "Suspected hooligan – have you seen this man?"'

Our laughter was cut short as reports came in on the TV monitors showing fighting on the beaches of Marseille where the game was being broadcast live on a giant screen. Groups of Tunisians had apparently attacked England supporters after Shearer's goal, throwing bottles. More fans had been stabbed. After the game we heard there were running battles on the city's Avenue du Prado. English cars, identified by their number-plates, had had their windows smashed. Oh, what fun it is to see the English play away.

The second-half kicked off to the sound of police sirens in the background. Why is it that every England fixture away from home has to be surrounded by a bloody war zone?

The game drifted on with the Tunisians clearly out of it. A moment of excitement came when Michael Owen stripped off his tracksuit and prepared to replace Teddy Sheringham as the crowd bayed, 'We want Owen! We want Owen!' You could imagine the watching world thinking, 'Who is this kid and what's all the fuss about?' All they knew was that Pelé rated him highly. With his first touch they found out why.

Owen zipped around the field and took on the Tunisians, running hard at the defence. He darted down the left flank, passed his man and thundered a shot past the keeper's post. It was wide of the mark but the speed of the move impressed. It spoke volumes about Owen's confidence. The eighteen-year-old was playing in a World Cup match and was clearly unfazed by the occasion. Bloody hell, he was some player!

Then Paul Ince surged forward and played what he thought would be a one-two with Paul Scholes. Scholes, however, turned on a sixpence, like Kenny Dalglish used to, and dug his right foot deep under the ball, scooping it into the air. Ince's expression of anger that he hadn't received the return pass was quickly replaced with one of delight as he realised the ball was going in for a goal. Scholes had scored one of the tournament's best goals so far. Hell, some of our fans might be arseholes, but we were showing the world we could play a bit. England 2, Tunisia 0.

Bobby Robson, commentating for ITV, said he thought England had played the best football in the tournament in the last twenty minutes of the first half and Terry Venables agreed that the most important thing was to get the win.

Chris Waddle described the performance against a 'very good Tunisian side' (*sic*) as excellent, while Lineker thought England had enough ability to progress well in the tournament. 'They're capable of pulling it off,' he claimed.

Guy Roux, the respected coach of the French club Auxerre, praised the England supporters in the ground and was impressed by what he described as England's 'power game'. French TV dismissed England as 'boring' and the worst of the rated teams in the World Cup. Well, you can't please everybody.

Glenn Hoddle knew how that felt. After the match every team's coach was obliged to hold a press conference in an area known as the 'mixed zone', usually a tent or mobile home close to wherever the players would leave the stadium.

The mixed zone swarmed with journalists, and getting a ticket to enter one of these things required breathtaking patience, pushiness or deviousness. I borrowed a ticket from a fellow scribbler.

Hoddle stood on a raised platform and chewed gum. He stared at his fingernails, occasionally shooting a look of disdain. He had all the countenance of a hooker at Pigalle, shagged out and itching for a ride home.

'I was delighted with the start made by the team,' he began. 'It was a very good performance and it was important to win. We could have scored more, but we won the game.' This would be translated by a short bloke in a suit into French and, where necessary, any other language. Behind him stood David Davies, the FA's media guru (who used to read out the final scores on *Grandstand* for the BBC, so he's been around a bit) who accepted questions from those he recognised in the English press.

'Alan Shearer's reputation goes before him,' said Hoddle in reply to a question about the captain's performance. I don't think he quite got the point. The press were disappointed in the team's performance, especially Shearer's. He hadn't created anything and had scored from a set-piece.

Hoddle, however, seemed to be ignoring his questioner's implied criticism. 'He had a limited number of chances, but he managed to score and that's what a world-class player can do,' he finished.

That seemed a bit rich. Sometimes you felt Hoddle said things just to please the jingoistic desires of sports editors. What was the point of having these question-and-answer sessions if the material never got above the intellectual grasp of a five-year-old?

'Any team has to attack from the back and defend from the front. All the so-called favourites have difficulties against this type of team.' (What, like a team with eleven players you mean?) 'They had limited chances and we created some - it's pleasing for a coach.

'The Tunisians gave one hundred per cent, which is all you can ask for as a coach. We played better than them on the day but, on any given day, any side can cause an upset. I'm delighted it didn't happen today.'

Bleary-eyed, a pressman popped the question we all wanted answered. Why hadn't Beckham played? Hoddle seethed with rage. He'd been talking tripe for twenty minutes but now the monotonous tone of his delivery was replaced by some real bluster. And about bloody time! 'I'm not here to discuss who played and who didn't with the likes of you!' he snarled. 'I'm pleased with Darren Anderton's performance [which was more than could be said for the rest of us] and the final result was that we played well and won!'

With that, Hoddle had had enough and he stormed off.

★

Alan Shearer was more at home with the press. He was so used to stonewalling them that anything remotely interesting he said was treated with reverential respect.

In the mixed zone, showered and changed, he had time to consider the implications of the first match.

'England put on a very good performance today, but it was the result that was more important than that. We can now spend the next few days in a more relaxed frame of mind.

'After scoring my goal I was obviously delighted. Paul Scholes's chances in the first half were hard to convert, so I was pleased that he managed to get a goal in the second half. If Paul had something to prove he did it today.'

Shearer was third favourite with the bookies to lift the Golden Boot award behind Ronaldo and Gabriel Batistuta and he was pleased with his goal.

'I know I've got high expectations placed on me, and scoring the first goal takes a bit of pressure off me. Everybody is saying that I'll score the goals that are needed if we are going to do well in the World Cup, and it was nice to get off the mark. I think you could say I was pleased. I had one chance and I put it away. That's from one game and it might take a bit of pressure off – until the next game at least. There is more to my game than goalscoring, but I'll go out to do my best to find the net.

'The most important thing is that we got off to a good start. I said the performance wasn't as important as the result, but if you can put the two together like we did then it gives everyone real confidence.

'We're in a good position in the group now and everyone is excited. But we mustn't get carried away with one result. We haven't qualified yet. The win over Tunisia was just the start, but we know we are a very good team and we feel sure that we can keep going.'

Shearer was also full of praise for the way that Hoddle had instilled self-belief into the players.

'That's part and parcel of him as a coach. He gives you the confidence you need. His job is to do that, to get it into the players and he does it really well.'

Shearer's goal meant that he and strike partner Teddy Sheringham had scored eighteen times between them in the fifteen games they'd been in tandem for England. But what did Shearer make of Owen's substitution in the last fifteen minutes of the game?

'Over a long period myself and Teddy have had a successful partnership, but if the manager wants to split us up then it's up to him. If that is the case then we know that Michael Owen will be ready to come in if he's given the opportunity.'

It was hardly a vote of confidence for Teddy.

Sol Campbell was modesty itself. 'I was just there to do a job,' he said. The big man from Tottenham had looked imperious in the match and was receiving plaudits from the minute he walked off the pitch. 'I made a couple of runs, but the space was there, and when you get the chance you've got to look to impose yourself on the opposition.

'You can't afford to think about the match, start worrying that it's the World Cup. Of course you're up against world-class players, but you've just got to go out and play the game.'

Tony Adams was just as delighted. 'I remember Euro '96, how nervous we were against Switzerland. First games are always difficult but you can't ask for more than a win and to get the first one under our belts.'

Gareth Southgate was being the funny man. The England players had a bet with each other about how many song titles they could get into their answers to TV questions. Asked about the leak of the team to face Tunisia, Southgate replied: 'Well, you always get a lot of careless whispers in football.'

England could afford to smile. They were on their way.

★

That evening I set off for the five-star Sofitel Hotel. It was set into the hills and had a panoramic view of the old port. It was where the England team had stayed, too.

I took a taxi there and dodged the pitched battles in the narrow streets. It was like a scene from a Keystone Cops movie, with Tunisians running one way and English running the other. The police didn't seem to have a clue who to go after, so they just hit out at everybody.

The taxi-driver was keen to take me to the birthplace of the king – *le roi* – Monsieur Cantona, who grew up in the suburbs surrounding the city. France's latest hero, Zinedine Zidane, hailed from Marseille as well but, much as I would have liked a guided tour, I had an appointment with England's brass band – well, Sheffield Wednesday's actually, but that's splitting hairs. A swanky meal and a jaunt round the harbour on a yacht were going to be thrown in.

Arriving at the hotel, it was as if I'd entered another world. Polished brass, gleaming mirrors, smart waiters and beer at a fiver a pop: I was in heaven.

Graham Kelly stood on the steps to the rear of the hotel puffing on a massive Cuban cigar. He was chatting to a couple of lads whose white England shirts hardly fitted in with the surroundings. I thought, 'Good on you, Kelly.' He may be a berk but at least he cared. He was hanging on to apologise to the Mayor of Marseille the next morning while the rest of the FA bigwigs had buggered off.

Police sirens continued to wail in the streets on the other side of the harbour, but here in the stillness of a warm night you could almost forget there was a war raging in the centre of the city. People were going to get hurt tonight.

I met up with the lads from the brass band but they were out of gas having blown their horn, if you'll pardon the expression, for the duration of the match. They set off to get some rest and I sauntered down to the harbour to catch my ride on the fancy yacht.

The next few hours were spent in the company of some gentlemen from *Loaded* magazine, an old pal Richard whom I hadn't seen for eight years and the sun-tanned skipper of our vessel – a Robert Kilroy-Silk lookalike – who had an interesting line in conspiracy theories. It was getting late as the latest twist on 'You realise that FIFA imports hooligans to sell coverage of the World Cup to TV. Violence sells . . .' echoed round the drinks cabinet on board, and I decided I'd had enough.

One taxi-ride home later, and bizarrely I found myself drinking with Bryan Robson and Viv Anderson in my hotel bar.

'Shouldn't you be at work?' I enquired of the *Eurosport* summariser, echoing the intro Des Lynam had tossed up for his opening delivery on the BBC that afternoon.

They said they'd moved hotels after having had enough of the noise from riots and fighting outside their own hotel by the old port. I wished them all the best, made an inquiry about Gary Pallister's move to Middlesbrough and hit the sack, full of booze and bizarre thoughts.

England had won and the Tunisians had gone down fighting. Graham Kelly liked fat Cubans and Bryan Robson had turned down the offer of Schnapps and a chance to stay up all night talking bollocks with members of England's barmy army. It had been a very long day.

*

The following morning I crept out of the hotel early to avoid the post-match hangover. The last thing I needed was to spend the day sharing cabs with potential hooligans on the way to the Gare de St-Charles. When I got to the station there were loads of tired England supporters, some of whom had slept rough on the concourse, while Frenchmen looked on in disgust. Unkempt and unwashed, England's travelling 'army' looked sorry and pathetic.

'*Les Hooligans se sont déjà déchaînés*', read the headline on *La Provence*, the region's daily newspaper. The Mayor of Marseille, Jean-Claude Gaudin, described the violence as a 'stain on the World Cup', and said the French state should lay on additional riot police and paramilitary units to tackle English hooliganism during the rest of the tournament. Marseille's police chief described English soccer thugs as 'drunken beasts', and blamed World Cup organisers for scheduling the match on a Monday. 'Are we always going to allow these hooligans to storm through all the sites of matches?' he asked.

*

Once aboard the TGV high-speed train to Paris, the fans chatted amongst themselves and many condemned the violence. Some though, were angry: 'We were set on by a bunch of fucking hairdressers. Fuckin' Tunisian scum. I can't go home and say I was beaten up by a fuckin' hairdresser, can I?'

The impact of what had happened didn't really hit home until we pulled into the Gare de Lyon in Paris just under five hours later. Gendarmes and soldiers wielding heavy machine-guns patrolled the platform, scrutinising our faces. God knows what would happen if there was any bother now. I just wanted to get out of there. I wanted to be anything other than English. For the next three days I refused to speak in anything but the broken French I was picking up. To speak my own language was simply too embarrassing.

As Paul Hayward of the *Daily Telegraph* wrote later on the subject of the English fans in France: 'If you can divorce this [the actions of so many thugs] from a game of football, say that it should all be forgotten the moment a ball is kicked, then your mental filing cabinet is stronger than mine.'

Pelé marked the fortieth anniversary of his World Cup début with a blistering attack on the hooligans, mercenary players and negative coaches. Did he have England in mind for all three, one wondered?

'These fans come to a game to fight, to cause trouble, to make war. This is disgusting,' he said. 'The police should act quickly to put these people in jail as an example to others because, until now, we've had a good World Cup with a lot of goals and a happy competition.'

Talking about coaches, Pelé was equally disdainful. 'What disappoints me most is the modern way of preparing teams. Many of the big coaches are afraid to play the beautiful game. The most important thing for them isn't to play to win, but to play not to lose.'

Back in La Baule, Glenn Hoddle could reflect on the events in Marseille. He claimed that some of the England supporters caught up in the trouble had been 'provoked' by Tunisian fans. There were two sides to every story, said Hoddle, and he praised the England fans who had cheered his team to victory. 'Inside the ground where I was there was no trouble. Every supporter who was there was fully behind England and they were superb,' he claimed.

All of them, that is, except for the nationalist bigots who sang 'No Surrender', and the arseholes who chanted 'Rule Britannia' during the minute's silence to mark the death of France '98 president Fernand Sastre.

'We saw clips that suggested that some of the England supporters were provoked, certainly down at the beach. Tunisian fans attacked them and there are all those facts to deal with,' Hoddle went on. 'Having said that, I was very disappointed with the hooligans and I was really upset by what I saw on TV, especially when some of them burned the Tunisian flag.'

Gareth Southgate was more forthright. 'What happened didn't affect us as players when we prepared for the Tunisian game. We just got on with the task in hand and did a professional job.

'But, as Englishmen, what happened off the pitch disgusted us. We were all very disappointed with what happened out there. It saddens me that these people have given us a bad name when thousands of well-mannered and well-behaved people gave us such a great reception during the match.

'There were people looking after us who took great pleasure from the fact that the country's name was being tarnished. It gave them a superior feeling. When we play abroad all we get are comments and knowing looks like "Your lot are a disgrace, aren't they?".

'It's up to the Government to take a tougher line. Only they can do it. The police have to be given the power to stop these people travelling abroad. Until they do, the problems will continue to exist. All this trouble is a social problem. Football is a vehicle on which it exists but it is a more deep-rooted problem than that.'

The trouble was the roots were taking hold. There was talk that if we saw anything like the scale of violence again in Toulouse, England could be thrown out of the World Cup. The FA were getting jittery about their 2006 World Cup bid, fearing for its safety. Typical! There were people travelling in France who were fearing for their *lives*. Shankly was wrong when he said football was more important than life or death. He was talking out of his arse. Or he was being misquoted.

CHAPTER SEVEN

The morning after

The England squad flew straight back to the north-west coast after the match. Those lucky enough to be working for national newspapers followed them in a separate plane. It was the first time an England World Cup campaign had split the players from the journalists and the writers were clearly cheesed off about it. Steven Howard from *The Sun* was moaning that his copy had been mislaid from that morning's edition of the paper and he looked quite comical as he cursed his way round the FA's press centre wearing shorts but no shirt. A blob of cream seemed to be hiding a blemish on his upper lip. Brian Woolnough's 'Woolie's Verdict' had disappeared too. *The Sun*'s new editor was away for the weekend and something had gone awry on the production front.

Every day at the training ground these boys were there. They'd been trudging round the world for years, trailing the nation's heroes and villains. I'd been with them in Tiblisi for the Georgia qualifier in November 1996. Several members of the press had gone out for a meal the night before the game and one of them had woken up with a fish in his pants the next day. He wasn't entirely clear-headed that morning but he thinks they were thrown out of the restaurant. They liked to enjoy themselves while they were away.

Tiblisi had been an eye-opener. I'd had breakfast in the team hotel; normally the press stayed in a different hotel from the squad but there was only one hotel in Tiblisi that wasn't ravaged by bullet-holes so we all mucked in together.

At breakfast, I ate my bacon and eggs with a short-haired Chelsea supporter who was intelligent and seemed to know all the journalists and some of the players. He'd been on all of England's recent away trips: 'When you're watching at home and the National Anthem starts, you get a lump in your throat and you know you should be there,' he told me. This sounded all very well until he started trying to offload a 'No Surrender' T-shirt to me.

Tiblisi was on its knees, a country ravaged by war and poverty. It was so run down even the yobs England brought with them were chastened by what they saw.

Harris, Winter and the boys were highly amused when we all squeezed into the press box that was no more than a wooden hut behind the players' bench. A brass band had sat down in front of us and started up a comedy performance featuring several less-than-notable renditions of Cole Porter tunes. Trying to phone copy instructions through to England had been a tricky task at that match.

Even though I'd been through experiences like Tiblisi with them, those boys would never acknowledge my presence. Magazines were looked down upon and freelance writers were the bottom of the pile. If you weren't working for a national you weren't worth bothering with.

So Harry Harris was still doing his thing for the *Mirror*. Woolnough and Howard for *The Sun*. Martin Samuel and Rob Shepherd *and* Paul McCarthy for the *Express*. Lee Clayton was there for *The Star*. Then there was the spooky spectre of John Sadler, the man who gave everything to you *straight*. For the broadsheets there was Henry Winter for the *Telegraph*, Glenn Moore for *The Independent*, David Lacey for *The Guardian* and Oliver Holt for *The Times*.

There were loads of them. TV crews for Sky Sports, the BBC, ITV and a host of foreign channels. You couldn't move for media people.

The FA had erected a marquee at La Baule that they kept stocked up with soft drinks and Press Association monitors that told us what was going on. Eurosport was broadcast on several TV screens and whenever they held a press conference, a catering crew would lay on some tucker. It was low-key but England *were* low-key. If it weren't for the fans you wouldn't know England were here. Hoddle liked to keep it that way.

After a light training session the coach plonked himself in front of the scribblers to give them his daily briefing. It was as if we were being fed scraps to lob back home. Something to enthrall the masses watching the footie on the telly back home.

No effort was made to discuss how things were going. Unlike previous incumbents in the job, Hoddle didn't see why he had to justify himself to the media. The FA were his paymasters and it was to them that he was responsible. Never mind the thousands of fans who'd trudged around the globe giving England their support. Our lads might be the most unsavoury bunch of football fans, but they got stuck in and gave their team a lift. Even in Tiblisi.

'Today's training was just for fun,' said Hoddle without a hint of humour. 'Tomorrow's will be the serious one. We've got a long road ahead of us and we have to take it one step at a time. Our main goal is to win. Our first victory, against Tunisia, was a good start to the Cup, but we can't judge much from one match. It will be easier to assess our potential at the end of the first round. Still, there were some really positive points about that first match, notably Paul Scholes's brilliant performance. He played very well and has become a key player in the squad.

'Every team has played its first match in this World Cup now, and we've seen how high the level is and how fast the matches are. Although there are thirty-two countries playing, it's obvious that there is no such thing as an easy match.'

Hoddle was satisfied with the team's performance against Tunisia but, unlike the tabloids, he wasn't going over the top. Instead he payed tribute to his captain, Alan Shearer. 'He's the best finisher I've ever seen.'

Hoddle allowed Shearer and Adams to sit out the day's training session with sore feet. Resting certain players from the open training sessions was a part of the cat-and-mouse game he was playing. The question was: did anyone care?

Journalists were left to wonder: where was so-and-so? Who was injured? If you didn't have much to write home about, this was all there was to discuss. Hoddle knew that was the case and was using the media to throw up a smokescreen around his players.

'Alan proved against Tunisia that he doesn't need five or six chances to score,' continued Hoddle. 'That's the touch of a true master, because he can score with just one chance.

'Alan is as good a finisher as I've ever seen or played with, and I think he can get better. He can score with his left foot, his right or his head, from inside the box or outside.

'Alan would be the first to say that his movement can still improve but so can everybody's, including Ronaldo. What's really important is that he's got off the mark and now he's scored early doors the confidence will be there. It means there's no pressure on him. That's off his shoulders, and even if he doesn't score against Romania he won't be worried.'

Shearer's willingness to undergo the ordeal by pain that is the lot of every top-class international striker was proved by his acceptance of the treatment he received from Tunisian captain Sami Trabelsi. 'He never moans, never comes off the pitch whining, although he does ask for decisions on the pitch,' said Hoddle. 'That's only right. The thing about Alan is that he's strong, which makes him such a hard man to mark. If you're marking him he'll give you a hard game, physically and mentally, but at the same time he's always in control.'

Hoddle was more upbeat than usual about his team's chances.

That's not to say that he didn't believe England could do well. On the contrary, he believed England could go all the way.

'We have a good feeling about us, and Alan is the figurehead of that. In training he's been as sharp as I've ever seen him. We held him back in Morocco, because we didn't want to show our hand. We were working quietly behind the scenes. That's the way to do it.'

Hoddle was excited that the players had got the first game of the tournament under their belts. He spoke of how eventful the journey back from the airport to the team hotel had been on the Monday night. 'A lot of the local French people came out to meet us,' he said. 'It was a controlled performance. We can play a lot better, but I've seen us start tournaments a lot worse.

'If some of the chances had gone in then we might have started with an explosion. I think you'd worry about that, but if we can make it a progressive thing I'll be happy with that.'

★

One man who wasn't feeling quite so upbeat was Teddy Sheringham. He'd failed to get on the scoresheet against Tunisia and been substituted by the prodigy Michael Owen. Sheringham admitted that he'd feared being axed from England's opener after his Portuguese nightclub antics in the build-up to France '98.

'I doubted I would start against Tunisia because of the trouble of the last couple of weeks. I had begun to wonder what would happen,' he said. 'I didn't feel at the time of the trouble that I had put my place in jeopardy but, with all the hullabaloo that came afterwards, I felt that I had.

'That feeling increased when England played a warm-up game behind closed doors against Caen in which Michael Owen started. I thought about it then. But it was a warm-up game, and you have to keep faith. I think you can only look at things in terms of football reasons and hope the manager looks at it from a football point of view.

'That's what he came up with. I didn't do myself any favours, and it was a relief when I was in the team. It was something I wanted badly.'

Sheringham spelled out his determination to hold on to his place despite the pressure coming from Michael Owen, who received a massive cheer from the England fans when he came on as a late substitute against Tunisia.

'Michael Owen is an outstanding talent. People want to see him play and rightly so. But I want to play for England and that for me acts as a massive spur.

'It's as simple as that, but you can't worry about who is in front or behind you in the pecking order. You just have to make the chance count if it comes along. I was quite pleased with my performance against Tunisia but there is need for improvement.'

Sheringham offered his thoughts on the predicament of his Manchester United colleague David Beckham.

'I know he has been down, but so would anyone who is not in the first eleven. Knowing his character, I know he will turn it on in training and when he does get his chance he will be better than ever. I am convinced of that. I know he is champing at the bit to play, and when you're dropped you want to do yourself justice and prove someone wrong. I've got no fears about him coming back and changing everything around.

'I was surprised he wasn't selected. He had played in all the qualifiers, but there are other excellent players in the squad.'

Sheringham reckoned Paul Scholes could be as influential as Paul Gascoigne in Italia '90.

'I thought he was outstanding against Tunisia and is a clever little player with a great understanding of the game. I was not surprised about how unfazed he was about such a big occasion and I don't think there is another player in the World Cup who plays the same way as he does and is such a threat in the box.

'I get asked about whether he has the potential to be as significant as Paul Gascoigne in 1990, when countries were not aware of him, and I think that is a good comparison.

'I've got every faith in Paul Scholes doing the business time and time again. But maybe to build him up like that now, and have all that sort of hype surrounding him, would be the wrong thing to do. It's not going too far to say he could be one of the stars in France.'

With that Sheringham was off. He was right about England having one of the stars of the tournament. But it would cost him his place to find out who it was.

CHAPTER EIGHT

The trouble with David...

Adidas were having a nightmare with their sponsored players. The French playmaker Zinedine Zidane, who, as giant advertising hoardings all over the country proclaimed, was 'Made in Marseille', had been sent off in the match against Saudi Arabia for stamping on his marker's chest. He would be suspended for two games. Patrick Kluivert, the maverick Dutch striker, had also been sent off for violent conduct, elbowing a player in Holland's match against Belgium. Alessandro Del Piero, the Italian superstar, hadn't even started a game yet for Italy. Worse still, David Beckham, the ace in the pack and the player Adidas had pinned most of their hopes on, hadn't kicked a ball in the tournament yet. The sportswear company had nervously laughed off any suggestion that there was a 'curse' on their players, saying, 'We are sure that at least one of these players will have a significant impact on the tournament.'

David Beckham was finding it hard to imagine he'd be making any impact whatsoever on the World Cup. Watching him train, practising his free-kicks and a move that involved lobbing the ball over defenders for Owen and Shearer to chase, you could sympathise with him. He hadn't taken Hoddle's decision to drop him from the England side well.

Assistant-coach John Gorman rushed into the press centre, all bustle and purpose, a bit like a movie director, only he had a whistle in his mouth instead of a microphone. Gorman gathered the ensemble in front of him and told us that Beckham would have 'some part to play in the tournament'.

A German reporter standing next to me asked, 'Who is this guy?' which made me chuckle.

Gorman was short and sported a bushy moustache. You could mistake him for one of the Mario brothers but he was so perennially cheery he'd be able to talk up the prospects of a romantic meal for two in the local Wimpy. Beckham was in the spotlight but the action was happening somewhere else.

An hour later, three England players were due to give press calls. David Davies, the FA's head of media, was happily chatting to select journalists, squashing stories that Hoddle and the press were falling out. Gorman was trying to encourage us – 'youse boys', as he called the media – to write nice things about England. Be upbeat and positive. One writer asked Davies how to spell 'youse'.

Graeme Le Saux agreed that while his attack play had been good up till now, he needed to concentrate on his defending. While he chatted to the top boys, Darren Anderton gave an interview over at the other side of the room. A dozen or so journos went to listen to him. I wondered how a player would feel if he was deemed so boring that no one would go and interview him. It could happen. Anderton insisted there was no friction between him and Beckham. 'David Beckham wished me all the best before the Tunisian game, so where's the friction?' asked Anderton. 'It's a twenty-two-man thing and we're all in it together. Everyone wants to play, you can understand that.'

Le Saux finished his interview as a blond, well-groomed lad wandered in on his own. Not for Beckham the hassle of being escorted everywhere by one of the FA's press officers. He stood quietly, waiting for his turn.

Sitting down to face what must have been upwards of thirty

reporters, Beckham revealed the 'hurt and shock' he felt after Hoddle opted to play Darren Anderton ahead of him on the right wing. He described how he had discovered his fate in front of all his team-mates when Hoddle announced the side on the Saturday before the Tunisia match. It was only an hour later that the stunned player was given the reason why he had not been picked. Beckham was frank and forthright in what he said and smiled meekly at the suggestion that he still had a part to play.

He had one final salvo, though. 'Can I just ask, which one of you is Graham Hunter?'

The boys bit their lips and cast glances at the fellow in the base-ball cap, screwed on back to front like a Yank, who was sitting in the middle row.

Hunter had written a disparaging piece about Beckham under the headline 'Sulky Spice' in that morning's *Daily Mail*, accusing Beckham of 'traipsing back to the dressing-room like a spoilt child whose ears were ringing from parental discipline at half-time'. Worse was to follow: 'His expensive Predator boots barely left the turf as he scuffed them along in obvious unhappiness. His shoulders were drooping almost as much as his bottom lip.' It was entertaining stuff.

Having nailed his man, Beckham looked his victim firmly in the eye like a disapproving guardian about to dish out his own brand of 'parental discipline' and said: 'You don't know me as a person so I wouldn't start judging me like you have.' Ouch.

Suitably chastened, Hunter joined the rest of the scribblers in the car park outside the press centre. 'That's fair enough, I suppose,' said Hunter. 'If you dish it out you've got to be able to take it yourself.'

The next morning we were granted our usual slot with the England coach. The tabloids had a sniff of a story: Beckham's clash with Hoddle, the star player and the manager falling out, was perfect cannon-fodder in the fight to flog a few more papers.

When Hoddle was asked if Beckham would, as Gorman had

indicated, play a part in France '98, he barked, 'I can't say that. I would be a fool to say one way or the other what is going to happen.'

Asked why he hadn't taken Beckham to one side to explain his decision, Hoddle was even more angry. 'If the players are going to be left out of the next game, then I will talk to them beforehand, but the Tunisian match was the first of the tournament for us. I didn't feel there was any justification talking to anyone as we went into the tournament. We had twenty-two players raring to play and there was not only David Beckham but other players left out of the starting line-up. As far as I was concerned I had to make a decision and then had to get on with working with the team at what was the right time in a closed training session.

'If David was frank in his interviews, then fine, but I didn't get that response from him when I spoke to David. He took on board everything I said and agreed with it. He wasn't in despair and his training has been fine since. I can only go on what happens when I speak to the player.'

When the newspaper boys gang up on big stories like this one was shaping up to be, they hound their quarry in packs. No one outside the inner circle of writers is allowed to ask a question for fear that the line of attack might be changed. The only crime worse than butting in is to leave your mobile phone on. Inevitably, some-one's started ringing just as the Q&A was hotting up. In this case it belonged to Nigel Clarke from the *Daily Mail*.

'Tut tut!' and 'Oh Nige!' went up the cries like a pack of school-kids at the back of the bus.

Hoddle was getting agitated by the relentless questioning and the antics of the press. 'There are twenty-two players available and I have been quite staggered that I have been asked about David Beckham. If we had lost 2–0 against Tunisia, and I had got it wrong, then there would be some justification. But we won 2–0 and won well.'

Hoddle looked stern and cast a disapproving gaze across the floor. He had a parting shot for his inquisitors before leaving.

'When was the last time David Beckham played on the right-hand side for England in the build-up to the World Cup? The answer is Portugal at Wembley in April. In the last few games he has played inside. There's your answer.'

And with that he was off.

*

David Seaman was having a quiet tournament. The thirty-four-year-old practised with fellow keepers Nigel Martyn and Tim Flowers under the supervision of former England stopper Ray Clemence. Clemence, like Peter Taylor, John Gorman and Hoddle, had played at Tottenham. The keepers practised stopping shots and jogged round the training pitch away from the rest of the players. Clemence liked to keep them concentrating on what they were doing.

Each keeper would take it in turns to stand in goal with his back to the others in the penalty area. On the shout of 'Turn!', he would have to swivel round and save the shot without having more than a second to see where it was coming from. Here at least we could argue we had the best in the world.

Seaman explained how much he needed to get everything right before starting a game.

'I make sure I wear a new pair of gloves for every match, so I've brought out enough pairs for all the games we might play and the training sessions,' said the big man.

'When it's as dry as it is out here they can flake a bit and I hate it when they've got any scruff on them. If there's the tiniest bit on one finger I won't wear them. I know the gloves are all right, but what if the ball hits that bit of the glove and it doesn't stick? If I pulled out a pair and it had the smallest mark on it I'd get a new pair out, just like that.'

He admitted he was a bag of nerves before going out at the Stade Vélodrome in Marseille the previous Monday. He also said he'd been up half the night playing the game over and over again in his mind.

The big Yorkshireman explained some of the superstitions we've come to expect from our goalkeepers. 'I won't wear the socks left in the dressing-room if they've got a pull in them. I also tape together the third and fourth fingers in my right hand, after I broke the fourth a few years ago.

'A lot of players have their little routines to go through but I've always believed you have to get the little details right. It's something I've developed over the years. After all, I couldn't wear new gloves when I was a kid – we didn't have them then!'

Seaman spoke of the similarities between Glenn Hoddle and Arsène Wenger. Wenger had been Hoddle's manager at Monaco and the latter had recommended Wenger for the post of director of football, later taken by Howard Wilkinson, a few years ago.

'There are a lot of similarities in the way they approach the job,' said Seaman. 'It's all about not being surprised by anything that happens on the park. If the other team has a guy that runs fast, you're stupid if you don't know it, you simply have to find out about these things.

'That's why we watch so many videos together,' said the goal-keeper, echoing what Tony Adams had said about maintaining a computer databank on each and every player. 'We study the opponents, their set-plays and how they defend against them, looking for any weaknesses we can exploit.'

Seaman accepted that his first taste of World Cup finals action was still a step into the unknown. 'I felt great after the game, but it was nerve-wracking before the start, very tense, and I know a lot of us felt the same.'

He admitted he had shouted his way into the game, with Highbury team-mate Tony Adams the chief recipient. 'He told me he wanted to get me going, so I gave him a rollicking,' said Seaman.

'He likes that sort of stuff but I know what I need and want on the pitch as well. It's about shouting the right things at certain times, and I need that. I have to feel right to pass on the comments to them.'

David Beckham once told me that he occasionally stayed up all night after a game, buzzing with excitement. Seaman revealed he'd had a similar experience. 'When we flew back here I was tired and wanted to get to bed, but I didn't finally drop off until after 3 a.m. That was because of the adrenaline, everything going through my head. It always happens, although never as late at that before.'

Despite the relatively sleepless night, Seaman was a happy man. 'We're feeling confident and now we've got time to prepare right for Romania,' he said.

★

The weekend before England's game against Romania in Toulouse I went to Paris to see Argentina take on Jamaica. The Reggae Boyz were expected to provide one of the stories from the World Cup but they were falling out with each other, and their manager.

René Simoes was a Brazilian who had achieved remarkable success with the Jamaicans, taking them all around the world to get to France '98. They had played to packed crowds in Kingston; one game drew more spectators than the crowd that turned up at Sabina Park to witness the brief appearance of the England cricket team in the First Test in the winter of 1997–98.

Here in France, Simoes had controversially included in his squad many English Premiership-based players who had played little part in qualifying. The squad was rife with politics and had split into various camps. Matters were not helped by the decision of the Jamaican FA to permit officials and management to bring their wives and girlfriends to France but not allow the same courtesy to the players. The players were also fed up with being confined to their hotel rooms. They felt that everyone else was in France to have a good time and that they were missing out on the party.

Waiting for our train to the Parc des Princes on the platform of the Trocadéro Metro station, just up from the Eiffel Tower, hundreds of brightly clad Jamaican fans had gathered, blowing whistles and dancing; their optimism at the prospect of an encounter with the mighty Argentina was a welcome relief in the heat and smells of the Parisian underground.

Across the platform, a troupe of French scouts marched in step, whistling '*Allez les Bleus*'. The national side's call to arms was taken up by voices all over the station as a friendly exchange of opinions was struck up between the locals and their visitors from the Caribbean.

The train pulled in. Every carriage was packed with the blue and white of Argentina. Boisterous but friendly, they welcomed the Jamaican fans onto the train as we set off for the Parc des Princes.

One of the Argentinians struck up the chorus of 'One Love', Bob Marley's impassioned plea for peace and unity across the world. It set the tone for a friendly trip out to the west of Paris and provided much amusement for the Rastas in our carriage.

Outside the stadium, touts were sneaking about as packs of Argentinians hounded them for tickets. The touts, French at this game unlike the predominantly English ones I'd seen at the opening match, were charging up to £350 for a ticket and were finding plenty of takers. When the gendarmes tried in vain to stop the touts from doing business they seemed to pick on Westerners; I saw at least three Americans being reprimanded for attempting to buy tickets.

Argentina hammered Jamaica 5–0 and Batistuta scored a hat-trick. They looked a different class from the side I'd watched from

The bizarre but colourful opening ceremony at the Stade de France was
followed by Brazil taking on the mighty Scotland

OPPOSITE PAGE: Tension was high in Marseille before and after England *v* Tunisia, but there was no trouble at the match itself

ABOVE: Colombian fans have not forgotten Andres Escobar; the Romanian band warms up for the game against England

David Beckham was both a hero and a villain, his superb goal against
Colombia not quite making up for his sending-off against Argentina
(photos © Allsport)

Two of the stars who shone most brightly for England, Michael Owen and Sol Campbell (photos © Allsport)

Vivid memories of France '98: two possible future French internationals show off their skills; the more typical well-behaved fans; and Alan Shearer unable to escape the media spotlight

a bar in Marseille. I overheard quite a few English voices muttering that if we messed up against Romania we could end up playing this lot in the next round.

★

On the eve of the game in Toulouse, Alex Ferguson dropped a minor bombshell on the England camp. He wrote a column in the *Sunday Times* criticising the decision to permit Beckham to attend the press call earlier in the week, claiming it was something he'd 'never have allowed'.

'Why was Beckham put forward for a mass interview with the media while he was still reeling from the shock of being left out of the team?' wrote the Manchester United manager. 'Those in charge of the squad's press arrangements should have considered that.'

This was interpreted as a direct attack on David Davies, the FA's media affairs officer; but, more satisfying for the reporters in Toulouse, it gave them some ammunition to have a go at Hoddle.

Ferguson then slated the England coach's decision to play Anderton ahead of Beckham. 'Beckham is just about the best crosser of the ball in British football and he would be more likely than Anderton to score. It isn't surprising that many have suggested Hoddle's preference for Anderton cannot be justified in purely football terms,' he wrote.

Ferguson was opening himself up for criticism by the press even though they agreed with everything he was saying. By his own nature, Ferguson doesn't endear himself to the media. He's fractious and has a low opinion of journalists. His having a pop at the England manager allowed the tabloids to kill two birds with one story and whip up the anti-Man United line while continuing to peddle their Hoddle's-got-it-wrong story. They were in heaven. You almost sensed the tabloids wanted England to lose to keep the story going.

*

On the Sunday evening Hoddle gave his last press conference before the match. He pinpointed Chelsea's Dan Petrescu, a player he himself had brought to Stamford Bridge for £2.3 million, as a major threat to England's chances. He rated the Romanian as the best right-wing-back in the Premiership, and observed that he 'pops up with important goals'. The contest would have added spice in that Petrescu would be marked by his Chelsea colleague, Graeme Le Saux.

Hoddle refused to be drawn at any length on Alex Ferguson's comments despite being asked three successive questions on the subject. He merely dismissed the criticism as 'not important', before adding, 'I have more important things on my mind at the moment, like winning our next game.

'I shall have an answer and a conclusion about Alex Ferguson after the match. It is something I am not going to get involved with now. I'm not concerned about what he has said. It is small talk. Talk to me about it after the match.

'I am focused on that and it does not worry me what people say. I would not be doing my job right if I worried about things like this. I have picked my side, so now let's get on with the game.'

*

The *préfet* of the Midi-Pyrenées region, Alain Bidou, announced measures to counteract any threat of hooliganism. 'What's difficult is to maintain a party spirit while making certain that safety is ensured,' he said. 'We also wish to keep up Toulouse's reputation for being a welcoming city.'

Answering questions on the general state of fear that reigned due to the early closing of bars (they had been told to shut at 11p.m.) and the postponement of the music festival (a giant annual street party a bit like the Notting Hill Carnival), M. Bidou insisted on the wise decision he had taken after consulting all interested parties.

Declaring that he wanted to 'trust all fans', the state representative emphasised that he had decided not to put up railings between the public and the pitch of the stadium 'because that would have been an insult to the enormous majority of non-aggressive English supporters who have come to see the match'.

The *préfet* then concluded with a thinly veiled warning to 'those who have less reasonable intentions; they won't be able to meet up with some of their friends who have already been imprisoned or deported after the incidents in Marseille'.

Bidou made it quite clear what would happen to hooligans in Toulouse: 'They have a choice: either go back to England or rest for a while . . . in the local jail!'

★

That evening England kicked off against Romania in the Stade de Toulouse. *The Sun*'s front page featured the berkish Tony Banks grinning like an old-age pensioner on D-Day under the headline 'Too Good Toulouse!'. Beckham and Owen, however, were once again on the bench.

The crowd were boisterous, filling all four sides of the stadium, singing 'No Surrender' and 'Rule Britannia', but at least there had been less trouble – though more arrests – than in Marseille.

Romania were tidy and passing the ball well, using all the experience of Hagi, their captain, to keep possession. From the start England were chasing the game and they had to keep a watchful eye on the dangerous Adrian Ilie up front.

After three minutes Hagi clattered into Paul Ince, leaving the Liverpool player limping. Minutes later the Romanian was booked for a tackle on Campbell. He and Ilie both had long-range shots at Seaman.

On thirty-three minutes David Beckham finally got his chance. Ince hadn't really recovered from that Hagi tackle and Beckham replaced him, moving into the centre of midfield. He looked wild-eyed, almost manic, desperate to prove his place in the side.

A minute into the second half and everything fell apart. Moldovan collected a pass from Hagi and slotted the ball past David Seaman. It was the first goal the keeper had conceded for England since Marcelo Salas had put two past him for Chile in February.

England lacked punch in front of goal. Sheringham was invisible and Shearer wasn't getting any decent service. Anderton was look-ing better on the wing but the constant attacking play from Romania was pegging him back, preventing him from getting crosses into the box.

After sixty minutes, Beckham narrowly missed and his shot was followed by efforts from Scholes and Anderton. Either Romania were running out of gas or England were at last finding their feet. They were clawing their way back into the game. Shearer had a shot saved and the crowd began baying for Owen to come on. After seventy-three minutes they got their wish. Teddy Sheringham trudged off the pitch to the obvious delight of the fans. You sensed he might have played his last match for England.

Immediately England were back at Romania, and even Tony Adams had a shot. Then, on seventy-nine minutes, Owen scored. The ricochet from the free-kick allowed the young player to slide in bravely between the keeper and the defence and smash home the equaliser. The whole stadium went mad. Up in the commentary box Kevin Keegan turned to Brian Moore and said, 'Only one team's going to win this now.'

And then Romania scored. Graeme Le Saux blundered a ball across his lines and, as he and Seaman scrambled to clear, Dan Petrescu, the player Hoddle had warned us about, sneaked in to slot the ball through Seaman's legs. We couldn't believe it. Seaman grinned in total disbelief and frustration. We could have throttled Le Saux.

Owen had one last chance and weaved his way through the defence but was unlucky to hit the foot of the post. Shearer had a shot saved but it wasn't to be. England 1, Romania 2.

★

After the game, Glenn Hoddle was in reflective mood. 'After coming back into the game, we are disappointed to lose at the end. But we gave away two sloppy goals and it cost us. At the end of the day, it was a stalemate situation, like a chess game.

'One of the positive points was Michael Owen's entry into the game and his goal. At 1–0 down and when you're a substitute, you have nothing to lose. I gave him a free run and told him to go out and enjoy himself.

'The Romanians are a very good side, but we didn't create ourselves a chance and gave away two sloppy goals. We kept them at bay but we had sloppy defending. We should have punished them, but they punished us, and we were disappointed. The next game will be decisive against Colombia who also have three points.

'It was a good win for them; they knew what to do. If we win or draw the next game, we qualify. The boys are disappointed about how we gave two goals away, but not with the way we played. If we play like that again, we'll win more games than we'll lose.'

In the mixed zone, as the players tried to make their way to the coach that would take them to the airport, reporters swarmed around, sensing that here at last was a story.

The tournament needed a shock, as you could sense the World Cup had just begun to slip from its high point at the start: too many teams, too many average games and not enough thrillers. The good teams were being drawn out and paired off against the developing nations. Even if there aren't any easy games left in international football, you'd still prefer to play Japan than Argentina, any day. So while we waited for Holland to play Italy or France to play Germany or Brazil to play Argentina, England *v* Romania was as good as it got. And England had lost.

Graeme Le Saux attempted to explain his poor defending. 'On the second goal, the forward punches me just when I'm tackling. He's got me off balance and I can't catch the ball. Afterwards he puts the ball between Seaman and me. It's really maddening; of course I do feel somewhat responsible.'

Michael Owen and Teddy Sheringham had mixed feelings too. Owen said: 'I'm happy to have scored but disappointed that we lost. But it is okay because we are going to qualify anyway.'

Sheringham was gloomier: 'I am not satisfied with the way I played. It was a good thing that I was taken out of the game and substituted by Owen. When a player isn't good, the public always wants to see someone else take his place. I don't question the decision even though it's something that no player likes. All the same, I feel great physically. The team played well anyway. We still have a match against Colombia to catch up in the group. If we put in the effort, we should beat them.'

Sol Campbell maintained that note: 'Despite the fact that we lost against Romania I still say we played well. The final score should have been different, anyway. Some people in the media have criticised our defence, but when your players have trained with the best European clubs they can adapt to whatever system the coach wants. After that, each player has his own qualities. As for the meeting with Colombia, we're pretty relaxed about it, even though we know it won't be easy. We've lost one battle, not the war. Anyway, beating Colombia isn't an end in itself – we want to go further than that in this tournament.'

Darren Anderton felt he'd proved the critics wrong with his performance: 'Since the beginning of this World Cup, I've had to prove that I deserve my place on the team. I'm pleased with the new responsibilities the coach has given me. My role is to block them from winning the ball back, without forgetting to add an offensive touch. Our defeat by Romania has dashed our hopes of finishing first in our group. But we're not going to draw against Colombia, we're going to win – to boost our confidence before we enter the second round.'

England flew back to La Baule that night. And with just four days to go before the match against Colombia in Lens, most people's thoughts were already turning to the likelihood of a second-round encounter with Argentina.

CHAPTER NINE

Time for some answers

The morning after the night before, everything felt like a blur. England had really buggered it up last night and I'd been on the road nonstop throughout the night to get back to La Baule from Toulouse. Watching England in France wasn't pretty, and the best course of action after a game was to get in your car and scarper. France was a beautiful country and it seemed a shame to spoil the picture by hanging about in towns closed down by hooligans or in the company of locals gripped by fear. The English had really left their mark on this World Cup, even if their football hadn't.

At the training ground only a handful of players were in sight. Will Smith's 'Summertime' and All Saints' 'Know Where It's At' blared out of the stereo as the sun shone down for the first time in weeks. This is all right, I thought, I'll just crack open a beer and take it easy.

Lee, Merse, Macca, Keown, Owen and the two Ferdinands were the only lads warming up. They loped along to the laid-back tunes while the press looked on, nonplussed. I didn't get it.

England lost last night!

Hello!

Is anybody out there?

Lacey and Nigel Clarke were discussing the team's tactics from last night. They didn't seem impressed. A ball was kicked over to where we were standing but no one moved to give it back.

'We've been told to stay off the pitch so we will,' chided Clarke.

Hoddle came over to retrieve the ball, but he didn't look any of us in the eye. Did he realise he'd screwed up?

Gary Newbon waddled around the journalists clutching a press release. He was doing the reports for ITV and fancied himself as something of a celebrity. Select journalists were pounced on in much the same way that he snatches interviews with players after a match and he whispered the latest findings on last night's ITV viewing figures: '19.4 million viewers,' he clucked. 'Third-highest figure of all time for England.'

We waited to be called in for our debriefing with Shearer and Hoddle. The senior men were going to do the talking. They realised the press wanted blood.

Shearer came in smiling. He's smaller than you expect and doesn't thrive on grand entrances. I think half the writers didn't realise he was there until an unusual hush descended on one side of the press room. They obviously hadn't seen him come in.

Asked what he thought of the team's performance, Shearer gave an honest and frank appraisal, from the captain's point of view: 'We're disappointed but we're not downhearted,' said the skipper.

Asked if he had any fears about playing Argentina if England beat Colombia – the more likely draw following last night's defeat – Shearer was upbeat. 'If you're going to win this thing [the World Cup] you've got to beat the likes of Argentina and Brazil to do it. I'm sure you lot sat in the stands last night and thought as we did that we can win this one after Michael scored,' he said.

He was particularly keen to comment on the massive vocal support the team had received and he had this message for the fans. 'We want to repay those fans. I've had one chance in two games and scored, which isn't bad.' And as for Michael Owen, he went on, 'The fans aren't daft, they know when it's right to bring someone on.'

Asked whether he thought Owen should have played from the start, Shearer was diplomatic: 'Managers are paid to make decisions like the one he'll have to make on Friday. Not only about Owen but about one or two others. I get paid to play football, he gets paid to make decisions like that.' He said he felt particularly for Teddy Sheringham but added, 'Every team that does well here has to have a bit of pace.' And as for David Beckham: 'David has done very well. I can understand his frustrations but he couldn't have done any more than he did last night.'

Shearer was then asked what the atmosphere had been like in the dressing-room after the match, at which point he surprised us: 'I had to go off and do one of those pee tests [drug tests] and I couldn't do it,' he grinned. His eyes narrowed to see if anyone was going to, er . . . take the piss. 'Have you ever tried doing one of those with some bloke standing over your shoulder?' he asked. No one in the room could admit they'd been subject to a drugs test – at least not a sporting one, anyway. 'I had to drink two and a half litres of water just to get going. I was up half the night on the loo,' finished the England captain.

Asked if he had a message for the fans back home on the eve of the match against Colombia, Shearer assumed his Churchillian stance: 'We should assume and we should believe.'

As we waited for Hoddle to come in and talk to us, some of the senior press boys mucked about on the stands. They seemed more at ease when England were doing badly – as if normal service had been resumed. Perhaps they felt there was less to write about if things were going well.

As word filtered through that Hoddle was walking down from the training pitch, one of them sat down behind the microphones and announced sarcastically: 'England's tactical genius is entering the building,' to hoots of hysterical laughter from the media ensemble. This was going to be a rough one.

'I'm looking at the balance of the team. I didn't feel at ease yesterday,' began Hoddle.

We were lined up in three rows of chairs in front of the England manager. David Davies sat to the left of Hoddle and stared at us, frowning. His face reflected the gravity of the situation. Davies had a massive head, and his blotchy face and wayward hairline made him look a bit spooky, like a squashed soufflée on a pair of shoulders. He had that newsreader's look of someone who imparted important information without necessarily knowing what it was he was saying.

For the first time in the campaign so far, Hoddle seemed to be on the back foot. Normally he'd bustle in, feed us a load of mumbo-jumbo and then be off. Today, though, it was as if he was waiting for the attacks and this seemed to have put him off his stride.

He wittered on about the defence ('There's a lot of goals being given away in those last few minutes of the match') and the team's adaptability ('Tony Adams holds the line together and we need his experience at this level. Our defenders are adaptable, they can play three at the back or four'). But it was Owen the papers wanted to talk about.

'I don't feel *bad*,' said Hoddle, ignoring them at first. 'I'd mind if the performance was poor but it wasn't. The first phase is the toughest yet. My belief has not altered at all. We're going to qualify. I thought we put in a good performance but gifted them two goals.'

Asked if he worried about the prospect of facing Argentina, Hoddle shrugged off the challenge. 'Why should we worry about Argentina? I'm positive. Last night I thought Darren Anderton was possibly our best player and I was pleased to see Owen come on and score. We asserted ourselves and we wanted to win it. Character and ability. You're asking me questions as if we're out of the tournament but I say this: if we keep performing like that we'll win more than we'll lose.'

The papers didn't share his optimism at the prospect of facing Argentina. We'd seen them demolish Jamaica and thought to remind Hoddle of his assertion that there were 'no easy games in international football'. Might one add, 'And certainly not if your team is England.'

The Sun's Brian Woolnough repeatedly asked Hoddle if he'd pick Owen in the starting line-up after his performance against the Romanians. 'Many people, myself included, think he should play,' said the journalist. 'So will you pick him?'

'I've always known in the third game you'd play off the back of what might have happened before. The third game is always an option,' answered Hoddle, as if the opinion of a burly tabloid hack was going to swing his decision one way or the other. 'You guys and the people back home will have to wait and see. It's my decision, I pick the side.'

Hoddle may pick the side, argued the tabloids, but *they* had to look after the interests of the millions of people back home who were hooked on England's progress. When the World Cup becomes the people's property, common sense goes out the window. Maybe we should hold a weekly lottery to decide which lucky players will get the nod this week. You got the feeling that the papers were never satisfied. But they were right about Beckham and Owen.

'I thought Darren Anderton played well,' continued Hoddle, irritated again. 'And I didn't hear any boos when Teddy Sheringham came off and I'll let Anderton do his talking with his boots. I've nursed Michael Owen for this and there was no pressure on him when he came on.'

Then *The Star's* Lee Clayton asked Hoddle if, having had time to reflect, he'd like to comment on what Alex Ferguson had written about Beckham being dropped.

'It's a bit disappointing. At the end of the day it's my decision who I pick. I won't lose any sleep over it,' was the curt reply.

Hoddle was reminded that he'd been asked to comment on Ferguson's team selection during Manchester United's European Champions' League earlier in the season, but had declined on the grounds that it was unfair on Fergie. 'He's doing the same job as me,' replied Hoddle. 'But it's unhelpful. Maybe I look at things differently,' he added, bitingly.

★

That evening I went to the press hotel, L'Hermitage, just behind the seafront on the other side of La Baule. I'd been invited to take part in one of the lads' early-morning kickabouts on the beach before but this was the first time I'd managed to get over to the hotel in the evening. Scotland were playing Morocco and they had to win if they were to have any chance of staying in the competition. The World Cup was finally reaching crunch time after what seemed like weeks of pussyfooting around.

The journalists were in the Green Flag room where a bar had been stocked up with free Carlsberg (another of Team England's sponsors) and a live feed for both BBC and ITV. Woolnough, the *Telegraph*'s Henry Winter and Oliver Holt from *The Times* were at the bar.

'Did you believe what he was saying about those injuries today?' said Holt, incredulously.

Hoddle had told us that Scholes had stud marks on his hand, Ince had a recurrence of an old ankle injury and that Sol Campbell had jarred his knee during training today.

'I mean, if he's got stud marks on his hand, how come it's wrapped in plaster?' continued Holt.

No one believed a word of what Hoddle had said, and I'm sure it was at this little get-together that the press boys decided to find out what was going on from within the England camp using mates in the squad. If Hoddle wasn't going to provide any straight answers the press would have to find out what was going on through other sources. The *entente cordiale* between Hoddle and the papers had come to an end. From now on, the gloves were off.

CHAPTER TEN

Hoddle's French connection

I'd gone over to Monaco with Glenn Hoddle for Manchester United's European Cup match earlier in the year. Peter Leaver, chief executive of the Premiership, had sat behind me on our tiny BA flight to Nice and when Hoddle walked down the aisle past him had rather embarrassingly started flapping his arms about cooing, 'Glenn, Glenn, over here!'

Hoddle looked rather out of step with the rest of the FA cronies. Howard Wilkinson bustled on board and took his place while the rest of the suits squashed into their seats like overweight tourists. Hoddle, in contrast, was all elegance: beautiful suit, small amount of hand-luggage, well groomed. He was the Europhile in a plane filled with old-fashioned Englishness. And he looked like he wanted to be somewhere else.

I remember seeing him hovering round the lounge of our plush hotel on the harbour front, chatting to a waiter in French, just looking for an excuse to disengage himself from the mob of English journalists, ex-players and fans who surrounded him.

'Whaddya reckon on this one?' asked a Man United fan in jeans, trainers and replica shirt. Hoddle smiled politely and went to sit down, only to be collared by Gary Newbon. You felt sorry for the guy in these conditions. Monaco was his patch and here he was surrounded by the very people he'd come here to get away from.

Glenn Hoddle had signed for Monaco FC on 12 June 1987, barely more than a month after Spurs' FA Cup final defeat against Coventry. David Pleat, his manager at Tottenham, had promised Hoddle that he would help him find a club abroad if he stayed for one more season, and he was true to his word.

The timing was perfect. Hoddle had spent fifteen years at Spurs and was fast approaching his thirtieth birthday. He was looking for new challenges and had grown tired of the carping and criticism about 'cultured' players – i.e. those who were considered a luxury in a game overrun by tacklers and hoofers. At the time of the move, Hoddle said: 'There have been times when I've felt I haven't been fully appreciated. It's all a question of the English mentality regarding a player of my type. That staggers me because there have been so few of us. I've always believed my ability will be better off on the Continent. Now I will need a different outlook as I step into a new beginning.'

Pleat let it be known to the European market that Hoddle was available towards the end of the 1986–87 season and the first club who showed an interest were Paris St Germain. Indeed, PSG, managed at that point by Gerard Houllier, thought they'd agreed a deal after sitting down for a meal with Pleat, Hoddle and the Spurs chairman, Irving Scholar.

It was Mark Hateley who swung the deal in Monaco's favour. He told his club's cerebral manager, Arsène Wenger, that the Spurs player was available and Wenger phoned Hoddle's agent (then, as now, Dennis Roach) to see if there was any chance of signing him. Following a conversation between Wenger and Scholar, the deal was done. It took ten minutes to seal it.

Hoddle and his young family discovered a world of immense wealth and extravagance when they arrived in Monaco. They flew there economy class but left as millionaires, because everything the player earned in the principality was tax-free. It was the transfer that changed him as a person and set him up for life.

Despite the lure of the high life, the Hoddles preferred to stay at home or go to church. Hoddle said later that Monaco was pleasant but artificial, full of 'plastic people living plastic lives'.

Arsène Wenger's reputation had been growing in France. He firmly believed in discipline and the need to be fit, both mentally and physically. Hoddle had never come across anything like it.

Discussing the player's skills and abilities with him, Wenger told Hoddle he wouldn't have to defend at Monaco. 'I want you to do the things you're good at. I want you to play in their half of the pitch and do damage in that area. I do not want you to chase back and tackle; that would just be a waste of your talent.' After years of slaving away on defensive duties in the English league, this was music to Hoddle's ears.

Colleagues described him as a quick learner and he very soon latched on to Wenger's ideas. The focus on diet, stretching and training paid off. Hoddle said that, at thirty-two, he felt in better shape than he had for ten years. Wenger advised Hoddle to lose weight so out went the diet of pies and lager and in came fish, pasta and salads. He lost a stone and at the same time increased his body strength. He was now the player Wenger wanted.

Hoddle's repayment to Monaco was immediate. In his first season the club won the French Championship and in his second Monaco finished third in the league and reached the quarter-finals of the European Cup and the final of the French Cup. Michel Platini, the former captain of France, paid tribute to him, saying: 'He is undoubtedly one of the best players to have played in France. Had he been French he would have won a hundred and fifty caps.' He won only fifty-three for England.

The idea of going into management didn't strike him until the early months of 1990, two and a half years after his arrival in France. A serious knee injury had kept him out of the game for six months and he used the time to reflect and write down his thoughts. It proved to be a cathartic experience.

'It's time English football took in some of the ideas from the Continent,' he wrote, 'I think I have something to offer, perhaps to players more than clubs. I'm sure I could learn from the mistakes my managers made with me. I think I'd be good for players.'

By the time Hoddle returned to England, he had changed completely as a person. Wenger's influence was massive, as the Frenchman himself recognised in Brian Woolnough's book on Glenn Hoddle: 'When a person is young, his outlook and perspective on life can be influenced, hopefully for the good. This is what happened to Glenn in Monaco. It was a good move for him for many reasons.

When Arsene Wenger was a young player he was influenced by a man called Hild at Strasbourg. A passionate character, Hild taught Wenger many of the details that the Frenchman was to now pass on to his maturing England player. Wenger's head was full of ideas and he believed that he and Hoddle had an understanding, one that might blossom as Hoddle's confidence in himself and his development as a person away from the pitch increased.

'It's good for the team when a player can transmit the ideas of the manager to the side,' said Wenger at the time. 'That happened with me and Hoddle and it had a good consequence for the side. From the start we had a good relationship. He was good at analysing situations and he was always ready to speak up about tactical problems.' As Hoddle reached his peak, the Liberian sensation, George Weah, joined the side. Immediately the predatory striker and the master of the well-timed pass struck up an intuitive partnership. Wenger reckoned that Weah would be given at least five chances of scoring by Hoddle in every match.

Wenger had sensed that Hoddle was uneasy with himself the moment he arrived in Monaco. It wasn't the strange surroundings that bothered the player but a realisation of the freedom he'd been missing back home. Something had always bothered Hoddle about the English system – predominantly 442 – and the demands it made on players like himself to be able to do everything, including tackling, when clearly his skills weren't suited for the role. Not getting a regular slot in the England team bothered him greatly and he had become disillusioned both with the English game and with his own ability to perform at the highest level.

'Without doubt he is the most skilful player I have ever worked with,' Wenger told the press. The Monaco manager was mesmerised by Hoddle's control of the ball and his perfect body balance. His skill in both feet was uncanny. Despite the close marking he received in France two men on him was never enough.

'I couldn't understand why he hadn't been appreciated in England. Perhaps he was a star in the wrong period, years ahead of his time. When I looked at the teams he played in and the players around him I thought he must have enjoyed it, but he clearly did not.'

Wenger immediately set about building the side around his man. The other players were happy to run for Hoddle and give him the ball because they knew that with one pass he could win them the game. He was also a prolific scorer and scored eighteen goals in Monaco's Championship year. Wenger now believes that Hoddle was a better player than he'd expected; a better player than the one he thought he had signed.

The lifestyle of the rich and famous on the south coast of France meant that everybody, including the males became more fastidious about their bodies. They took greater care of themselves, which meant less fat and more exercise. Hoddle was in the best shape of his career. 'The culture and way of life had a big effect on him,' said Wenger who believed that Hoddle had finally found what he had been searching for.

Three years after arriving in Monaco, faced with a crippling knee injury that his Strasbourg specialists said could take anything between three months and a year to heal, Hoddle began thinking about becoming a player-coach. Yet even then the doubts remained. It was Wenger who spotted the latent managerial ability in him. 'What impressed me most was his analysis of the game. His intellectual ability to have an opinion and defend it well. And he had the determination to follow through an idea. He had the ability within himself but he wasn't convinced of the importance of football in his life,' said Wenger. 'Not until he was injured.'

Hoddle admits that without Wenger he would never have made the decision to take the manager's job at Swindon, gone on to Chelsea and from there to coach England. At his first press conference as manager of the national side, he said: 'Without Arsène Wenger I would not be here today. I owe him a lot. Monaco was a vital part of my life. I will never forget it and am grateful for what I learned there and what I discovered about myself.'

Having found what he was looking for in France, Hoddle returned to England in 1991. Chelsea engaged him as a non-contract player so that he could use their facilities to regain his fitness. After playing his comeback game in the Chelsea reserves he announced: 'We've got the talent to stand beside the best in Europe, but it's not expressed properly.'

Just days later an offer came through on the phone and he was able to put his theories and everything he had learned in France to the test ... with Swindon.

CHAPTER ELEVEN

Ghost town

I drove from La Baule to Paris on the Wednesday night. The front of my car had been torn off in a parking accident the details of which I won't bore you with, but the result was I had to attach the bumper to the rest of the vehicle using two rolls of gaffer tape. Quite what Ford were going to make of it when I got home was something I tried not to dwell on as I bombed along the N31 at 90mph.

Spending too much time with the England camp can make you stir crazy so I resolved that *if* I made it to Paris I'd go and see the Brazilians train. Their training camp at Ozoir-La-Ferrière was a forty-five-minute journey out of Paris. Unlike the English FA at La Baule, the Brazilians had laid on a huge welcoming party for the thousands of fans, reporters and curious onlookers who came to visit every day. To ease their passage the village was renamed 'Ozoir-Brasil' and signposted from all the main autoroutes. A huge marquee was stocked up with food and drink for the throng and a band struck up a samba beat while spectators sat in specially erected stands to watch their heroes train.

Whenever Ronaldo got the ball a huge 'Wow!' filled the air. I was harder to please. I thought Ronaldo and Edmundo did bugger

all. Their tricks rarely worked and they looked lethargic, dis-
interested, bored.

Once upon a time Terry Fenwick said that being with
England was boring. Bobby Robson had responded: 'I tell you
what. He's on about being bored – I bet he's bored now with a
broken leg. I bet he's sitting at home thinking, fuckin' hell . . .
'cos life is a bore, isn't it? The guy who works in a factory, who's
mixing the cement, or lugging the bricks – it's a bore, isn't it?
And he's saying it was a bore playing for England 'cos there was
nothing to do?'

Could Ronaldo *really* be bored? Despite scoring two goals
against Chile, Brazil's national paper *O Globo* had produced a
reader's poll which voted him the second-worst player of the
match. Brazil, like England, had already lost one game . . . and no
side had gone on to win the World Cup after suffering a first-
round defeat since Brazil themselves in 1958.

As Alan Shearer had said earlier in the week, the fans weren't
stupid. The Brazilian supporters could see something was wrong
with their hero. Was he injured? Was he coping with the huge
pressure and expectation placed on him? Or was there really
something seriously wrong with him . . .?

★

That evening I went for a meal at Le Reminet, a wonderful
restaurant behind Nôtre Dame on the left bank. I washed down
the snails and *foie gras* with a rumbustious bottle of Pinot Noir,
having decided I should treat myself since Lens was going to be a
drink-free zone from tomorrow morning onwards.

The build-up to England's game against Colombia in Lens was
always likely to be surrounded by troublemakers. German thugs
had already put one unfortunate policeman, Daniel Nivel, in

hospital; he would still be in a coma when the final whistle blew on the World Cup. .

The locals weren't about to take any chances with *les hooligans anglais* and many had boarded up their windows and skipped town. The police were geared up for a massive operation to foil the worst of the trouble, and anyone driving into Lens was stopped and refused entry if they were found to be carrying excessive amounts of alcohol.

While it was hard to shake off the gloomy feeling that once again England had scarred the World Cup (even if no hooligans turned up in Lens, being forced to close down an entire town just to play a game of football is outrageous), there was some good news: Owen and Beckham were both going to play from the start.

★

On the eve of the most important game of his career so far, the England coach sounded like a man in control of his destiny, dealing comfortably with a barrage of questions, most of them pertaining to the side's two young stars. At one point a Canadian journalist asked: 'If Michael Owen was The Beatles and Teddy Sheringham the Rolling Stones, whose tune would you be whistling in the shower in the morning?'

Hoddle smiled and replied: 'I've always liked the Beach Boys.'

He revealed a few injury concerns: 'Paul Ince's ankle is still a problem, Paul Scholes has a sore back and Sol Campbell has a tight hamstring.' But only Gareth Southgate was definitely out. 'Gareth's improving all the time but he's going to be just a little bit short for this game,' said Hoddle.

Campbell's injury had already changed once this week as had Scholes's. Wasn't it his hand that was hurting a few days ago?

Despite the doubts over whether Hoddle was telling us everything, relations with the press were cordial. The animosity that had flared up earlier in the week had subsided in the face of tomorrow's crucial game. Hoddle was relishing the challenge. 'The bigger the game, the more we find out about our players,' he said. 'The bigger the match in the past, the better we've done. With the qualifying game in Poland, we got it right. In Rome it was a similar scenario. We came up trumps on the night. We know what the country wants. If we lose here we're packing our bags. But there's no fear in the camp.'

Steve McManaman, Owen's club colleague, was upbeat about the youngster. 'When he receives the ball, the first thing he does is go at people with pace. A lot of players don't do that. He does and that excites people. He's the type of player who can go at a defender and beat them, rather than be with his back to goal, lay the ball back and go and find another position. Pace is very important. You see some very average players but they've got pace and they are dangerous.'

With the skilful Tino Asprilla out of the Colombian side – he'd been sent home after alleging that there were 'several players who should have been substituted before I was' following his side's opener with Romania – the threat to England had been reduced. Surely we wouldn't muck this one up.

★

The drive north to Lens took me an hour and a half from Paris. At each motorway toll gendarmes stood by the gates, peering through car windows, searching for signs of booze. They were an imposing crew with their boots laced up to the calfs, their machine-pistols and berets. They looked like tooled-up members of the cast of *Thunderbirds*.

As I drew nearer to Lens, more and more GB number plates

sped past me. The flag of St George was often to be seen draped over the rear window in the customary football-fan fashion. It was like a marauding army descending on the former battlefields of northern France; a place where so many lives had been so pointlessly lost in the First World War.

On 1 July 1916, the British and French forces had launched the Battle of the Somme to relieve the pressure on the French troops defending Verdun. The front ran roughly north-west to south-east, six kilometres east of Albert across the valley of the Ancre and over the almost treeless high ground north of the Somme – huge hedgeless wheatfields now, their monotony relieved by an undulation as slow as the rhythm of a long sea swell. These windy open hills had no intrinsic value, nor was there any long-term strategic objective – the region around Albert was chosen simply because it was where the two Allied armies met.

There were 57,000 British casualties on the first day alone, approximately 20,000 of them dead, making it the costliest defeat the British Army has ever suffered. Sir Douglas Haig is the usual scapegoat for the tragedy of the Somme, as seen in the *Blackadder* series, yet he was only following the military thinking of the day. As the eminent historian A.J.P. Taylor put it: 'Defence was mechanised, attack was not.' Machine-guns were far more efficient, barbed wire more effective, and, most important of all, rail lines could move defensive reserves far faster than the attacking army could march. The often ineffectual heavy preliminary bombardment favoured by both sides only made matters worse, since the shells forewarned the enemy of imminent attack and churned the trenches into a giant muddy quagmire.

Despite the bloody disaster of the first day, the battle wore on until bad weather in November made further attacks impossible. The cost of this futile struggle were 415,000 British, 195,000 French and around 600,000 German casualties.

It was difficult to put the history of this place to the back of your mind. The flat fields were a reminder of the pain and suffering that this part of the world had already endured. England's fans had better not make matters worse.

★

Lens was a ghost town. Pulling off the road to Calais, dipping through miles of open countryside where there was nothing to see save the unusual sight of a solitary train station plonked in the middle of the former battlefields of the Somme, we passed Arras and arrived at England's final first-round destination.

The only people on the streets of Lens were England supporters. Most of them were wearing the pitiful expression that comes with hours of travelling on a whim and a prayer without a ticket for the match.

After all the carnage and misery English fans had left behind them in Marseille and Toulouse it was hard to feel any sympathy for an England fan without a ticket.

The red-brick houses made the place feel like Legoland and gave it a very British air. Back-to-back estates had been built after the bombing in the Second World War and the gloomy weather simply enhanced the feeling that we were in Milton Keynes or some other ghastly modern English town. It certainly didn't feel like France, and seemed almost as though we'd been sectioned off, deposited in weird isolation away from the gaiety of the World Cup to see if the Colombians could finish us off, clear us out before we polluted the rest of the tournament.

Scotland supporters had spoken earlier that week about the need for self-policing. It was time England did the same. A few mindless scum, shitheads who claimed their actions were patriotic, were tarnishing the reputation of Englishmen throughout the world. If the true England fans – the ones who sing louder than any other, who'll travel further than any other and who'll put up with more grief than most – if those same supporters aren't prepared to say 'Enough is enough, we don't want your kind here', then sod 'em.

If England's supporters can't be relied upon to behave themselves like decent, civilised human beings when they travel abroad then don't invite them to the party. Kick England out of international football. Lock all the morons into a cage and let the British Boxing Board promote the ensuing riots as entertainment – only available on the satellite channels, of course.

All we needed in Lens was some billowing tumbleweed, the whiff of gunpowder and a cigar-chewing hero to complete the Spaghetti Western scenario. Sergio Leone couldn't have come up with a better set.

CHAPTER TWELVE

Now we're getting somewhere

Paul Ince was nursing a fractured ankle. We only discovered this after the World Cup had ended but here in Lens he was talking up his role as chief tackler, the man you had to get past to score. Since the big cheeses had decided to up the ante and get the refs to order players off willy-nilly, Ince was in danger of finishing the match in an early bath. Was he worried about the refereeing?

'Before the tournament started, we thought there would be red cards left, right and centre, and then all of a sudden that wasn't the case,' said Ince. Then Michel Platini and Sepp Blatter said something and suddenly the referees started handing out cards for fun.

'Glenn Hoddle talked to me in Spain and explained how important it was for me to stay on my feet. I said to him that it wasn't a problem as far as I was concerned. I'm a hard tackler but a fair tackler. Four or five years ago it might have been a problem when I was a bit rash. Since I've played in Italy I've learned to stay on my feet.'

The Liverpool captain sounded calm and assured, the senior pro at the heart of England's midfield. Did he envisage any circumstances when he might dive in? 'If you were getting beaten 2–0, and you can see the game slipping away because someone "did" one of your team-mates with a bad tackle, you might go for it then. It can happen. If the game is going the way you want it to go, I can't see any of our lads getting sent off. It's the biggest tournament in my life. It's a dream to be in it. You don't want to ruin it with one silly piece of madness.'

Ince's words echoed round the training-ground as the rest of the squad prepared for Colombia. Someone would make a mistake in this tournament and, as the advert said: 'One man will be remembered for what he did with his feet.'

As Ince had come off against Romania to make way for Beckham's starring role in midfield, it looked certain that either he or Batty would have to make way for the impish young whippet from Old Trafford. And so it proved. David Beckham was feeling far more relaxed. He'd got the nod that he would be starting tonight's match in place of the unfortunate David Batty. Owen was playing, too.

In the media centre hundreds of reporters gathered to gawp at pictures of beautiful television pundits telling the boys why they fancied David Beckham and what they'd give to be in Victoria Adams's shoes.

At the same time, however, stories had started to circulate that German hooligans had been stopped outside Lille, following reports that they were intent on seeing who was 'top dog' with the English. One reporter insisted that the police had found two hand-grenades on the Germans.

At the bar, Trevor Brooking, Big Ron, Ray Stubbs and John Motson were exchanging commentary tips as Peter Beardsley breezed in to join them.

As I'd entered the stadium's perimeters a grown man dressed up as a baby whizzed about the place spraying water at people from his pram. If anything could incite a riot, he could. A bunch of

Morris Dancers pranced in the ridiculous manner of a West Country bumpkin in front of a bemused audience while a brass band played up to the crowds.

Colombians, some of them wearing the number 2 shirt of Andres Escobar, the player who was murdered after Colombia's exit from USA '94, mingled freely with the English supporters.

Graham Kelly was spotted chatting to fans before he entered the VIP area. He was always out and about, as if he craved the loathing of the football-going public who have no time for his mono-syllabic utterances and protestations of innocence every time English football gets a bum deal.

There was an atmosphere of uncertainty about the place. Was there really a possibility that England could be knocked out?

In the surrounding streets things were somewhat different. Eighty English thugs were arrested before the match as drunken idiots 'shamed the nation' once again. Louts went on booze-fuelled rampages as hundreds of hooligans defied the alcohol bans. Black-market sellers were doing a roaring trade in the side streets away from the watchful eyes of the police as fans made arrangements to watch the match in bars which would then be locked shut.

The trigger that sparked the violence was a bottle hurled through the passenger window of a Frenchwoman's car. As she drove off in terror, a hundred French CRS riot police arrived in a convoy of dark blue vans. They lined up to face the yobs and, wielding batons, charged towards them under a hail of beer bottles and full cans of lager. Snatch squads moved in to arrest at least half a dozen England supporters. It was reported later that the hooligans' ringleaders were moving among the ranks, inciting the thugs to take on the police: 'There are forty thousand Englishmen here and only a thousand French police. We can't let them give us a doing,' one of them shouted.

More than thirty people were arrested during the clashes. André Dellon, deputy commander of police in Lens, said: 'Some of the English behaved like animals. Their behaviour has been very different from that of the German hooligans, but the result has been much the same.'

Bottle-throwing skirmishes flared in the nearby city of Lille as thousands of English fans walked straight off the train and into bars. The local authorities tried to enforce an alcohol ban but some bar owners wanted to cash in. English voices chanted: 'If it wasn't for us you'd be Krauts,' just as they had in Marseille.

In Ostend, hundreds of English hooligans caused mayhem during a three-hour spree of drunken violence as they went on the rampage. They picked fights and used bricks to wreck two police cars. It seemed that no matter what tactics the authorities tried, nothing could stop the English thug from having his day. If things carried on like this, we'd be thrown out, with no need to even play Colombia.

*

I sat in a tiny garden to the rear of the media centre as the press boys gulped down bottles of red wine. The alcohol ban was supposed to cover a fifty-kilometre radius from the ground but here, just yards from the stadium doors, they were knocking back the local plonk. It didn't seem right somehow.

Roy Hodgson, Blackburn's manager, gave TV interviews behind us. He'd been all over France during the World Cup checking out the players. He'd done all this before as Switzerland's manager at USA '94 and the press seemed to like him.

Just before the match started, we took the long walk up to our seats. The four stands at the Félix Bollaert Stadium were steep, similar to those we were familiar with at home and, unlike the town of Lens itself, the atmosphere was pleasant.

England supporters held sway on all four sides as we'd come to expect and they roared their approval when the names Michael

Owen and David Beckham were read out as the team was announced over the Tannoy.

The sportswriters covering the match were handed a notice before kick-off. 'At the end of the match journalists who would like to collect photos of HRH the Prince of Wales and HRH Prince Harry will be able to do so at the Fuji stand,' it read. 'Photos will be taken of Prince Charles and his son when they arrive and also during the game.'

Whoopee! I thought. The Prince had come straight off the TGV to the rear of the stadium and into the ground. I wonder if he clocked any of the violence?

Hairs stood up on the back of my neck as the National Anthem was played. TV monitors in front of us showed the two princes standing proudly, soaking up the passion overflowing from the crowd. It was going to be one of those nights. I didn't fancy the Colombians' chances.

After six minutes Owen had his first shot. Up until then the Colombians had been stroking the ball around quite nicely. They didn't have any pace but they knew how to keep possession.

There were gasps as Seaman mis-kicked a clearance and nearly let Colombia in, but apart from that early scare the South Americans looked unlikely to trouble our net, even if they had more of the ball.

On nine minutes Anderton crossed for Shearer but the captain missed his shot. Two minutes later Beckham hit a ball first time into the danger area but Shearer again nodded just wide.

Ten minutes later Le Saux made another dodgy mistake in defence and let Fredie Rincon through on the right, only for the mighty Sol Campbell to cover back and tackle.

Just then the television director switched the coverage on our overhead monitors to Paris – Tunisia had just gone 1–0 up against Romania! A penalty. If that score stayed as it was and England won this match, we'd avoid Argentina!

The Romanian players looked bizarre as they buzzed around

the field. Every single one of them, bar the bald goalkeeper, had dyed his hair bright yellow. Apparently they had made a bet with their manager before the start of the World Cup that they'd bleach their hair if they got through to the last sixteen. Qualification having been secured by beating England, the players kept their side of the bargain while their manager, Anghel Iordanescu, shaved his head.

Romania looked ridiculous and it was impossible to tell who was who. When I finally made out Hagi, he looked like an overweight wrestling freak. Jimmy Hill said he reckoned it was a ploy to help the players spot each other on the pitch, making passing easier; but the Tunisians, who couldn't beat an egg, had gone 1–0 up. I could hardly believe what I was seeing.

I switched my attention back to the match unfolding on the field below me. On nineteen minutes Graeme Le Saux missed an open goal but less than sixty seconds later the ball fell to Darren Anderton in the six-yard box and he blasted it into the roof of the net. It was a really stunning strike. England 1, Colombia 0.

A couple of minutes after the restart, Colombia won a free-kick. Paul Scholes refused to withdraw the requisite ten yards and was booked. Not long after, Michael Owen shot over the bar and then, on twenty-nine minutes, Paul Ince carried the ball upfield and won a free-kick in a dangerous area.

I turned to my mate, Scott Morgan, who was sitting next to me and asked, 'Beckham territory?'

He's a Man United fan and agreed that it was just far enough out for Beckham to get the ball to dip over the wall. 'I've seen him score loads from there,' said Scott.

Beckham grabbed the ball, placed it on the spot and you knew there was only one thing going through his mind. Memories of his free-kicks against Chelsea and Liverpool were filling my head and I reckoned he'd go for the top left-hand corner. I curled my notes up into a tight ball and waited expectantly.

The ball sailed through the air and flashed past the wall.

Mondragon dived to his right but had absolutely no chance. It's in! It was Beckham's first goal for his country. What a moment for the twenty-three-year-old.

He ran towards the touchline and dropped on his haunches, punching the air in front of him with both fists, unloading a double-barrel of emotion. The fans in the stand in front of him erupted and kicked off a conga as Beckham collapsed under a sea of team-mates.

The game restarted but the conga continued on the top tier of the stand to my right. The stewards looked on, unsure what to make of it. The fearsome England fans known only for their violence were at last showing some of the humour that you need to get through a lifetime of watching England play.

'Let's all have a disco!'

The hymn from *The Dambusters* started up, rolling over us like a sea of emotion, the waves crashing relentlessly on the pitch. The players were strolling around the field, full of belief. Scholes had a first-time effort saved, Shearer tried to head in a first-time cross from Anderton and Scholes's scissor-kick went just over the bar. End of the first half.

Owen started off the second half with a shot on target and then, on fifty-six minutes, Sol Campbell picked the ball up on his own penalty area and strode forward in the manner of Alan Hansen. The pitch seemed to open up in front of him and so he continued his way up field. No one was coming to tackle him, he was going to go all the way! Memories of John Barnes in the Maracanã stadium against Brazil and Maradona against our lot flooded in, and Campbell looked like he was on the verge of scoring one of the greatest goals of all time. The stadium paused, holding its breath. The Colombians had completely frozen. Only Campbell seemed aware of the possibility. Normally, you remember only glimpses, the odd flash of moments like these, but I can still picture every stride. Frame by frame. Campbell looked to his left and to his right and thought, 'Should I pass?' It was that moment of indecision that thwarted him. Valencia cut him down, seconds before he released a shot and the opportunity was gone.

'Let's all have disco, la la la la, la la la la . . .'

Behind the Colombian goal the England substitutes were warming up. Les Ferdinand and Steve McManaman were relaxed enough to stop and sign autographs. Ferdinand posed for photos as proud dads snapped him and their sons together. It's the last image I have of the game, and it's one of the best memories of the entire World Cup. I appreciated that, Les.

The whistle blows and it's England 2, Colombia 0. Even though the Romanians have clawed one back to draw with Tunisia, meaning it's Argentina next for our boys, right now we could take on the world.

★

As I got up from my seat in the stands, I saw an old twat from one of the papers shove past one of the volunteer helpers, the girls who speak perfect English and show you to your seat – stuff that's kind of important if you're an ignorant old git who can't speak the lingo. 'Why don't you get out of the way, always standing about,' he huffed disgracefully. He had all the manners and charm of one of the thugs in the streets of Lens.

In the media loos, Big Ron Atkinson stood waiting for a cubicle, mobile phone held to his ear, shades on, suntanned as ever. If he wasn't such a legend you could easily mistake him for one of those second-hand car dealers who's made it big on the Costa del Sol. But big respect to the man: he's given us terrific entertainment and he plays his part all the way down the line. There's nothing quite as important as self-importance, and there's a lot of that in football.

In the lift on the way down to the mixed zone, Paddy Barclay from the *Sunday Telegraph* summed up the evening. 'We must have had twenty or thirty shots on goal this evening,' he said in his Scottish brogue. 'If Germany had played like that, we'd be saying, "Bloody hell, who's going to stop them?" But we blew it against Romania.'

There was a terrific scrum inside the mixed zone. Ray Clemence walked past me whistling 'Three Lions', which would have horrified Hoddle – he has always felt the song identified England with his predecessor, Terry Venables. You couldn't blame Clemence, though. It filled the entire stadium for most of the second half.

Again we had an interminably long wait for Hoddle to come along and answer the first question. The Colombian coach had been and gone, announcing his retirement. Asked who he fancied to win the Cup, he had replied: 'Well, England and Romania are both good teams, but then there's Brazil and the hosts, France. Italy and Argentina and Germany have all won it and I've liked the look of the Dutch . . .' In other words, anyone who was left. He had as much of a clue as the rest of us but, as Clint Eastwood once said: 'Opinions are like arseholes and everyone's got one.'

It was well past eleven o'clock by the time Hoddle finally made his way up on to the podium. He'd been to the England dressing-room, discarded the white polo-shirt that he'd worn during the game and replaced it with a bright red one. He looked cool, bright and satisfied.

'The team played very well tonight, they passed the ball well and the defending was excellent. We controlled the match from beginning to end. The long balls from Beckham to Owen and Shearer went very well and David scored with a superb free-kick. But all the players did well in this match. You can only be happy when each player rates an eight out of ten score. But we won't get big-headed; tomorrow we'll have to start thinking about Argentina. My only worries are Paul Ince's injury – he's got a cut on the shin – and Paul Scholes's yellow card.'

As Hoddle rumbled through the rest of the evening's play, the journalists' eyes drifted towards the screen behind him. A bored French TV cameraman in the stadium, unaware that he was still on the air, had turned his lens on an attractive female official. Gradually, as Hoddle told us about Sol and big Tony, the camera's attention focused tightly on a particular part of her anatomy. At the precise second that the coach's voice announced that 'at this moment in time the lads have done well', a huge roar went up in the room.

Later in the session Hoddle was asked about the performances of Owen and Beckham. He could smell the thinly veiled criticism that he should have put them on them earlier in the match against Romania. 'Coming into this tournament we watched Colombia closely and we earmarked David Beckham and Michael Owen for this game. Colombia play with a flat back four, with the full-backs sometimes in front of the centre-halves, so we needed pace because the space was over the back.

'David Beckham can play the ball over the back and obviously with young Michael's pace and Alan Shearer's pace, that is what we were looking to do, and I think we did that excellently.'

Journalists looked on in disbelief as Hoddle attempted to claim back some of the ground that had been lost earlier in the week when he'd suggested that the two golden boys of English football needed breaking in to the World Cup gently. As far as the press were concerned, England were verging on the hopeless without these two, so their attitude was 'get them in and let's see what happens'. Hoddle hadn't gone along with this and now we were facing Argentina, one of the favourites, when we could have been playing Croatia, considered by many to be lightweights in comparison.

'We spoke about this earlier today,' said Hoddle, 'and we wanted Argentina. I feel we're better when we play against a big football country, better against a team like Argentina. We wanted it to be them rather than Croatia, because the people back home would expect us to beat countries like Croatia.'

So that makes sense. Shearer had said the fans weren't stupid but

Hoddle reckoned that a match against Argentina was better than one against Croatia. Because the opposition were bigger. Well, excuse me, but surely it's all to do with motivation, and, while I appreciate these boys are all being paid millions of pounds for kicking a cow's bladder round a field, if they can't get motivated to win a World Cup then they should piss off and let someone else try. And surely motivating players is part of *your* job, Mr Hoddle. The man was talking gibberish. But the man had won.

'We never had any doubt about qualifying. We never felt the performance against Romania was poor,' he was saying.

One interviewer asserted that there was a bulldog spirit in the side. 'That was in the fans,' Hoddle replied. 'Tonight there wasn't a bulldog spirit in the team, tonight was a class act.'

Hoddle allowed himself a moment's respite from the duty of revealing nothing. After all, he's got a book to write same as the rest of us. 'It's a lovely feeling as a coach. I don't know why, but I just knew David was going to put that ball in the back of the net before he took the free-kick. I felt the distance was right, that the keeper was standing in the right place. I just had such a strong feeling, and when it happened it was fantastic for the lad and for the team.'

The hour was fast approaching midnight and the tape-recorders were being switched off. Compliments were payed to Hoddle as he walked away from the throng. 'Brilliant stuff, Glenn,' muttered the boys who were slagging him off just three days earlier.

★

The players rushed through the maze in the mixed zone to get away from the stadium. There were hundreds of reporters in there and they all wanted a slice of the lads. Macca waltzed past us, barking, 'No!' rather brusquely when asked for a word. Steve doesn't rate journalists and he may have a point there, but players shouldn't sink to our level. After all, we're creating the hype that helps them secure ridiculously huge wage packets. You can't have it both ways, boys.

Beckham wouldn't say boo to a goose so it's no surprise when he stumbles through the throng. He does at least spare us a brief word: 'I was really confident going into this game against Colombia. I was very focused before the kick-off because I knew I had to prove myself. People expect a lot from me. The coach gave me specific instructions for the match and I'm proud of having proved up to it and also for having scored the goal that sealed England's win.'

Paul Merson and Rio Ferdinand stopped for a few moments to speak to their favourite writers, but it was left to the skipper to dish out most of the comment. Shearer was becoming a really pleasant man to do business with.

'I'm not disappointed at not having scored,' he grinned. 'My partnership with Michael Owen went well. He's really going to be a great player of the future; he's certainly going to become one of the best footballers in the world. England can win the World Cup even if it's not the best team at the moment. But if we want to win, we've got to be capable of beating everyone, including Argentina. I think they are definitely among the favourites for the title and they've beaten everyone they've played so far. But the other side's style of play doesn't matter. We have to play our own game and control the match like we did against Colombia. But we won't get big-headed – we have to remember that we've already lost one game in this World Cup.'

Sol Campbell was already looking forward to the next match: 'Now it's going to be really tough,' he admitted. 'The Argentinians are very strong. We defended well tonight and Anderton and Beckham scored two fabulous goals. We won't prepare ourselves in any particular way, though. We've just got to stay focused. It's all very well saying that we're going to win the World Cup but first of all we've got to think about the next game. We'll take each match as it comes.'

Michael Owen was obviously delighted: 'The game against Argentina will be a real chance for us to take revenge for 1986. It's just a childhood memory for me but the goal that Diego Maradona scored with his left hand sticks in my mind. It'll be a difficult match because Argentina are a good side.'

And with that they were gone. The players were having the night off, a chance to catch up with their wives and girlfriends at the fourteenth-century chateau at St Omer, a well-deserved rest before the big match in St Etienne next Tuesday.

★

The drive back from Lens to Paris was hazardous. Fans, drunk on nothing more than delight in victory, stuck out thumbs as they ambled in a well-behaved fashion towards the north. They'd walk all the way to England after a performance like that.

Scott and I compared notes on the players. 'What about Campbell, what about Adams!' We couldn't think of a single poor player in the team. This was a side that could take on anyone.

For an hour and a half we nattered away. As the lights on the motorway loomed up and sped past us we knew we'd made it safely back to Paris. The thought occurred to us that maybe, just maybe, we really could beat the Argies.

We were exhausted by the time we finally crashed out at half past two in the morning. Nothing seemed to be open in Paris at that time of night. But we were happy.

CHAPTER THIRTEEN

A weekend in Paris

'This is fucked. This is well fucked!' These are my thoughts as I'm standing in a queue, biting my nails down to the quick, waiting for the Woman in Green to get rid of the fat bastard at the front of the line.

I'm here to plead my case. My beef is that I've applied for the wrong game and now I can't get a ticket for England *v* Argentina. I was told I could reconsider my selection, but you know how it is. One person tells you one thing and another person tells you something else . . . So I've ended up with a ticket for Romania *v* Croatia. And who wants to watch that? Not me, and I can't see many takers.

The bloke in front is a sweaty bald bastard. Just look at him. He's barking on about not having a ticket for a game he probably doesn't even want to see, arsehole! 'It's Brazil *v* Chile, and you haven't given out any tickets to the British press,' the guy is saying. 'I mean, who the fuck are some of these people? – "The *Nigerian Gazette*", "*O Media*" – what's all that about? What about the British national press? Don't we get a look in?'

The Woman in Green is understanding. She sympathises. She can see his point. She's tapping her fingers and thumbing her papers but there's bugger all she can do about it. The French ticketing system has ground to a halt. It has reached an impasse. It is deceased. It is no more.

There are twelve thousand journalists covering the World Cup, most of them here in Paris, and they all want a ticket.

You see, the French organisers thought that after the first round, after sixteen teams had buggered off, there might be an easing-up in the queue, a slacking-off in the system. Some of these people might sod off back to wherever they came from and leave the big boys to get on with it. But oh no.

Put it this way. If you had a pass to the biggest sporting event in the world and you could get into games if you were cunning enough and crash on people's floors or stay in any one of the cheap hotels in the more run-down *arrondissements* of Paris, what would you do? That's right. You'd bloody well sit tight.

So whereas before, those twelve thousand journalists had forty-eight games to split between them, now there are only sixteen left (if you include the third-place play-off which, in my opinion, is a farce). No one's going home and every Tom, Dick and Harry is after a ticket, whether they're from *The Sun* or the *Timbucktoo Express*.

'I see there's a ticket for *The Guardian*,' says the Woman in Green, with the mildest jolt of sarcasm.

'Oh well, that'll please their three readers,' says the fat man, picking up the tone in the woman's voice. 'Look, I'll come back, but can you *please* try to sort me out a ticket,' he finishes, a modicum of civility in his voice.

'Next!'

'Er, yes, well, you see, I've put in a request for the game in Bordeaux, thinking England would be there, and, er . . . you do speak English, don't you? Er, yes . . . well, the thing is, they're not playing there, are they, they're in St Etienne, so, well, is there any chance I can change my ticket?'

'No.'

'Oh. Why not?'

The Woman in Green who, I can now see from the name badge stuck on her right breast, goes by the name of Colette, is chain smoking. 'This is all bollocks,' she's thinking. 'These fucking English bastards, can't speak French, expect the world, and here I am, working a fourteen-hour day, arseing around trying to find them tickets. Well, screw you.'

I can't blame her for thinking this. I'm reminded of Michel Platini's praise for *les bonnes vertes*. 'No organising committee, whether it be the World Cup or the Olympic Games, would be complete without the help of the volunteers. They are absolutely essential.'

These poor bastards are here from eight in the morning till midnight every day, constantly answering questions and sorting out problems for people like me. One bloke in Bordeaux put up a pal of mine for the night. He'd seen him crashed out under his computer and had hauled him off home, even though he'd never seen him before in his life. *And* he gave him breakfast the following morning.

The volunteer recruitment programme began in October 1996 and finished a year later. The CFO decided to use local people for each of the ten venues and their selection committee targeted specific groups within each community: football and sports associations, universities and colleges and France '98 commercial affiliates. 'No large-scale recruitment campaign was launched as we didn't want to end up with a lot of very disappointed candidates,' said Max Bouchett-Virette, head of the volunteer programme. They deserved everything that came their way.

Back to Colette . . .

'You have no ticket for St Etienne, so you must swap,' she's saying to me. Swap, oh yeah, I'm really going to be able to swap. If I can find someone mad enough to cough up their best seat in the house in exchange for entry into a match even the TV cameras can't be bothered with.

'Hey, anyone out there care to swap my lousy ticket for the East

European derby featuring a bunch of Klingons against the rejects from the Hair Bear Bunch in exchange for your ticket to see the clash of the round?'

'Any Eastern European hacks round here?'

'Any loonies?'

For fuck's sake!

There is nothing Colette can do. Like the fat man from the tabloids, I'll just have to wait and see. Colette tells me she'll be in St Etienne on Tuesday and will try and sort out something for me down there. I don't fancy my chances, but I give her my mobile phone number just in case.

★

I go and sift through the day's newspapers and grab a coffee. To my right I see Sepp Blatter, the newly elected President of FIFA, chatting away. Earlier in the month I'd seen him on television; just as he was receiving the grateful thanks of a collection of admiring goons, he collapsed in a heap of Armani, his legs swept beneath him as though someone had pulled the rug from under his feet.

But now he's back, holding his first proper press conference, the most powerful man in football beaming out to the rest of us via a bank of fifty TV screens. He's answering questions on the CFO's ticket policy for the next round (what ticket policy?), hooligans and the plight of Japanese fans who've been ripped off in a massive ticket-sales fraud back home. No one asks him about the football. Welcome to the world, Mr Blatter.

Football's really got very little to do with all this when you think about it. France '98 is all about money and corporate bollocks. It's diseased, and the sixteenth World Cup is just the start of what's developing into a cancer football can't ignore.

Watching Blatter blether, his bald crown sweating under the profusion of lights, the rows of TV crews and snappers in front of him, the shady men in dark suits on his flanks I think to myself, what's this all about? Just who is this game for?

The fans? You *are* joking.

The players? Well, they get paid plenty, but they're being used as meat. The Romans called them gladiators, didn't they?

The football directors? Well, if you mean the shady blokes in dark suits, those goons who surround Blatter, then yes. What are they called in *The X-Files*? 'The Syndicate'. Yeah, that's them.

And, behind it all, in the shadows, is the man who controls the biggest buttons . . . the TV *mogul*. He's your Cancer Man. He's the Top Dog. The man in the black hat.

Oh, you don't reckon? Well, try telling me what the real fan felt worked about this World Cup. Ask the fans how they felt about paying through the nose to see a game, being forced to buy tickets from touts with scrawny English accents; about paying through the nose for a shirt; about paying through the nose to traipse around France. Who's made a killing out of the football?

And when it's all finished and we settle down for the rest of the summer, what happens next?

The big clubs aren't making enough money, the poor blighters, so they want a 'super league'. A league where no one gets relegated. A league where you and I fork out to fly around Europe or pay to watch it on the box.

Who wants this? Not you or me. But those shady men in dark suits, they're sitting back, watching the cash roll in. They know we'll support our teams come what may. We'll follow them into the cesspit. Oh yes. Those shady bastards are having a laugh. And the joke's on you and me.

Cancer Man has got it all figured out. We'll be pay-per-view football freaks forking out fifteen quid to watch a game on TV before the year 2000. He'll have already worked out a plan and you can bet we'll be buying season-tickets for the fucking telly in the next millennium.

And I still haven't got a ticket for England *v* Argentina.

★

I left the Centre de Media International in the Porte de Versailles on the outskirts of Paris and headed back into town. The city was lit up by a brilliant blue sky, the sun gearing itself up for the long day ahead.

Gorgeous girls filed past me in that way that gorgeous girls do. People with looks and money. People who are used to being people that other people stare at and desire.

I notice a girl eyeing up a soldier at the train station. He was holding on to the barrel of his machine-gun like it was his own pride and joy, and she was flicking her Bambi eyes at him and pouting her lips, lips you could roll cigars with. He nodded in recognition, eyes taut, chin erect, stiffening his grip on the barrel. She walked on, wiggling her arse, giggling to her friend and thinking of the possibilities.

Paris was alive with sexual feeling. There was electricity in the air and that evening the Brazilians were playing Chile at the Parc des Princes. It was good to be alive.

I headed for the Gare du Nord to meet my girlfriend off the Eurostar. It takes less than three hours from Waterloo to reach the centre of Paris and it's so simple to use. I could feel a whole different world opening up for me after a month of the TGV and now the Eurostar. Train travel is the way forward, my friends.

Brazilian fans, clad in that ubiquitous yellow shirt, that omni-present yellow shirt that even I'd gone out and bought, filled the streets and the station. Families and friends greeted each other off the trains.

Porters were carrying luggage for the well-dressed and well-heeled. Old ladies, with hats and pearl necklaces, sporting pastel-coloured skirts worn down below the knee, directed the porters to waiting cars. Maybe they're the only ones sensible enough to ask for assistance. Maybe our generation simply isn't sussed when it comes to asking for help – 'No, it's all right, mate. I can manage.'

It was a busy Saturday morning in Paris. There was no evil menace, none of the stuff I'd felt the last time I was at a train station. Not like the time I came off the train from Marseille. Being English was okay once again.

I felt brave enough to converse in French and didn't get embarrassed if I got it wrong. It was all right if people sussed I was *one of them*. One of those English chaps. There was clearly a world of difference between me, who was getting by in the local lingo nicely, thank you very much for asking, and the tattooed chaps to my right by the sandwich vendor who were just breaking open the first can of Stella at half ten in the morning. Straight off the boat then, boys?

At the station I met my girlfriend, who always seems to be at the back of the queue, and we headed off to the hotel. After freshening up, we went for a beer at the Metro Brasserie across the street.

Scott, the lad I went to Lens with, was sitting at a table on the pavement, tucking into a mountain of mussels. He looked pale and tired after yesterday evening's happy times and four weeks on the road seemed to be taking its toll on him, but give him a beer and a bowl of *moules* and he's happy.

To his left were two Frenchmen with bleached blond hair, one of them sporting a stripy blue-and-white Breton sailor top. They were drinking chilled champagne and sucking on Havanas. Every time a good-looking girl walked past – which was often – they'd spin her a line, whistle and give her marks out of ten. And they say romance is dead.

Scott told me they were football fans, singing '*Allez Les Bleus*' at odd intervals, but why were they here? And what were they celebrating? Certainly it was the first time I'd seen a board outside this brasserie advertising football on TV.

I was starting to sense that the mood in France was changing. The locals were beginning to 'get' the World Cup. The French team looked good in the qualifying stages and they were certainly in with a shout of winning the thing. I felt I was really starting to feel a part of the local culture, so I sat back and soaked up the atmosphere. Even the waiter recognised me.

*

That evening we took a stroll on the left bank of the Seine. Romance was in the air. I could almost touch it. We could hear jazz music in the background, the swishing of soft cotton dresses in a warm breeze. In the darkness couples held hands and caressed, lit up only by the light of a yellow cab glimmering off the river. There was the sound of bongos and nomadic chanting as travellers and hippies played out the soundtrack to a Saturday night in Paris.

We passed the restaurant boats behind Nôtre-Dame, swayed by the coachloads of American tourists and found a quiet street and a wonderful restaurant.

Up by the Hôtel de Ville a giant screen played out the drama of that evening's match. There were thousands of ticketless Brazilians and a good selection of Chileans, but for the first time there also seemed to be a fair number of locals as well. I'd already watched a handful of games from here but this was the first time I'd really seen Paris come alive to the *Coupe du Monde*.

Ronaldo was all over them. His sidestep on the run was by now a feature of the World Cup. It was a brilliant piece of skill that was reminiscent of a Samurai swordsman, swishing his blade back and forth, from behind one ear, over to the other, before delivering the fatal blow.

Ronaldo and co hammered Chile 4–1 and the Brazilians danced in the streets. They were joined by lambada-ing Nigerians and Danes who were due to meet in Paris the following day. The world's nations had come out to dance and there was a grin on the face of France. It felt like the World Cup had kicked off for real.

★

The next day we got up late and lay in bed watching Sky News. A grave-faced man with orange skin gave us the morning's headlines. He and his pretty female sidekick exchanged flippant remarks about football. It wasn't quite Rooster Cockburn and Katharine Hepburn, but I took what I could get overseas. Reports from St Etienne showed a town shaking in its boots at the prospect of an English invasion. A slight blonde reporter, who'd braved the battle-lines and given us daily reports of how the troops were doing in the fields of France, today revealed all was quiet on the western front. The customary drinks ban might not be enforced because the local gendarmes reckoned they'd take their chances with our boys. Brave lads.

We kicked off the day with a few drinks at the brasserie. I was getting on like a house on fire with those guys in their penguin suits, even when they asked me if I'd mind them spending an evening with the good lady. France are to play Paraguay. Of course, I'd forgotten. You just sort of assumed that France were going to beat teams like Paraguay.

In the bar young tykes chatted and flirted and smoked heavily while up by the TV screens some of the local gentry gathered, watching the football. It seemed strange that the youngsters weren't as bothered as the grown-ups.

A blue-rinsed woman wearing far too much make-up and

jewellery spits out some words at me that I took to be pidgin English.

'*Oui, je voudrais l'équipe Française, c'est une bonne chance*,' I replied in kind. It seemed to do the trick because she smiled and turned her attention back to the screen. Her teeth rattled with excitement every time Djorkaeff got a half-chance.

At the end of the first half we left them to it. I had to drop my girlfriend off at the Gare du Nord. If this was London and England were playing, can you imagine the streets busy, thronging with shoppers? No, nor can I. But here in Paris, even though I could tell people were watching in the bars, there were still loads of locals wandering about, oblivious to what was unfolding in Lens, where this afternoon's drama was taking place.

In a bar outside the station a rowdy bunch of young French lads were singing loudly. '*Allez les Bleus! Allez les Bleus!*'

A nonchalant barman took our order. The match had now gone way past normal time, so how come they were still playing? The tray-carrying penguin explained that France had failed to score at least ten sitters and now the match had gone to extra time and they were looking for a golden goal. Blimey! It was tight.

I could see grown men clinging on to their beers like it was their mothers' apron-strings. Any tighter and that Stella's going to shatter, sunshine.

This was more like it. A game of footie reducing grown men to tears. I was starting to worry that French blokes didn't care.

And when Laurent Blanc finally scored I swear the whole of Paris erupted.

Every bar in the street teemed with excitable Frenchmen and women. They were hugging each other. Christ, they were even hugging the waiters. The most miserable men in Paris raised a smile. I saw the back of a police van open its doors on the other side of the road and watched dumbfounded as a dozen gendarmes jumped out, grinning like fat cats. They'd got a tiny monitor in there and had been watching along with everyone else.

The tension that preceded that fumbled goal from Blanc and the knowledge that this win was enough to take France to the quarter-finals is, my friends, what galvanises a nation. This was the moment when so much of what was to follow really began. Paris was drowning in a sea of champagne that night, and for the first time you could sense the fizz was coming back into the football.

CHAPTER FOURTEEN

Journey's end

The south-bound TGV which I caught from the Gare du Lyon was a double-decker affair. With staircases, toilets and a bar between each compartment, it felt a bit like travelling in a swish maisonette on wheels. On board were tourists and foreign TV crews but no England supporters. I don't know why this should have been so. There just weren't any.

The journey itself was uneventful and I passed the time thinking about the England press call the night before. The squad would probably have left Nantes and be flying down to the Andrézieux-Bouthéon airport by now, I mused. Quick shower and then a spot of training in the afternoon. I hoped I'd make it.

Paul Scholes was confident of success. The whole squad were. The Colombia result had lifted the nation's spirits but the players in La Baule had always believed in their ability: 'We managed to find ourselves better against Colombia. Qualifying for the second round is just one step. We have players who can make the difference,' he said. 'Argentina is a painful memory for the English. Personally, I admit I was upset by Maradona's handball in the 1986 World Cup. When we play Daniel Passarella's team, we have to watch out for Gabriel Batistuta's speed and ability to win the ball.

When I see the quality of our attackers, though, I'm very confident. We shouldn't forget that Argentina are the favourites in this meeting and so they'll be under more pressure than us.'

Shearer agreed that the Fiorentina striker was the main threat but he shared Scholes's confidence. 'One could say we are even calm about this match. We'll have to stop Batistuta but if we can achieve this then all is possible and the winner of the match will be in a good place to reach the final.

'People are still talking about the famous 1986 match, but we're not here for revenge – and, anyway, none of today's players are directly concerned. At that time I was sixteen years old and on holiday. I was just disappointed by the result, that's all.'

After the players came the boss. Hoddle had to shove his way through the film crews and photographers that cluttered up the entrance to the FA's media centre but once he'd sat down he was calmness personified: 'I am very satisfied with the way we played against Colombia,' he told us. 'In particular, the way we circulated the ball was much smoother. This system has enabled my players to score at least two goals per match.'

He was effusive in his praise for Owen and Beckham: 'Young David does nick the ball, that's why he can play inside as well as wide. He knows when to lay off people and when to close them down as they're receiving the ball. This is a part of his game which is getting stronger and stronger.'

As for Owen, Hoddle was pleased with the prodigy's ability to absorb advice. 'We were urging him to go across the line of the defender, which he did,' said the coach of Owen's startling break against Colombia which had been halted only by Jorge Bermudez. 'To be fair, the defender got in a terrific tackle. But Owen did the right thing. He knew he wasn't going to get a shot in. It was interesting to see a young lad do what he should have done. A penalty might have been given. I tell players, "If you get knocked, go down." Why should we let them have eighteen free-kicks and we only get five? That's what they do to us.

'Going back to the first round, I noticed that all the big guns had a few lapses: Brazil and England both lost a match, Germany and Italy both struggled. Only France remain unbeaten after the first round. So we're going to approach this second round cautiously, but confidently. We know Argentina have some real fighters, who are able to get control of the game and then speed it up suddenly.'

But now we had Owen and he was the quickest man in France.

★

Once the train got to Lyon, I waited ten minutes for a local service to St Etienne, where England were due to take on Argentina. The sun was baking the station concourse. There were quite a few England fans milling about but they looked like they'd just arrived in France. Their skin was pale and their Umbro England shirts clean.

On board the one-stop ride to St Etienne, I overheard four young lads from the north chatting excitedly about where best to stay. 'Lyon's got more nightlife and I hear St Etienne's a shithole,' said one big lad with close-cropped blond hair, England team shirt, shorts and trainers. His companions all looked the same.

A suntanned passenger in the seat opposite the boys spoke up. He sounded like the cricket coach David Lloyd who, I gather, is from Lancashire. 'Actually, it's been brilliant these last few days,' he told them, enthused. 'The locals have been really hospitable and there's a giant screen where you can watch the footie. The French game yesterday was tremendous, all the barmen where giving us free drink after they won. Terrific!'

The freshers grinned at the prospect of free booze. Their tone was friendly and their talk was neither coarse nor racist nor sexist, unlike so many of the 'lads' I'd had the displeasure of meeting on my excursions around France. The women on the train, who were suspicious of the boys at first, sat back and relaxed, reassured that these *anglais* weren't hooligans.

★

Getting to St Etienne took about forty-five minutes from Lyon. The temperature was noticeably hotter than in Paris and it took me a little time to adjust my breathing, there was so little oxygen in the air.

I'd arrived in St Etienne without a ticket for the match, still hoping that Colette would be able to sort out something for me, and I'd forgotten to book somewhere to stay.

I made enquiries at the tourist office but got nowhere until I told the blonde assistant in a low-cut floral dress, just enough to reveal a cleavage, that I was a journalist – '*J'écris pour la presse anglaise.*' She directed me to a France '98 organiser's booth and suggested I try my luck with the dark-haired gentleman there. He recommended a short hop in a taxi to the Media Accreditation Centre which was bolted onto the Geoffroy-Guichard stadium. There were people there who could help.

Outside the stadium four lads loitered by the taxi rank. They poked their heads through the window of my ride almost before the car had stopped. 'How much for the station, mate?' asked one.

I could tell the driver didn't like the look of these blokes with their tattoos and grubby shirts, and he pretended to *parler* no *anglais*. I helped out with my limited vocabulary.

In order to get into the media centre I had to go through a series of body and baggage checks. After the metal detector gave me the all-clear I made my way through a throng of journalists to the accommodation desk where a peroxide blonde in a tight brown skirt and high heels grinned and asked if she could help.

After much telephoning, form-filling and flirting, we came up with a place for me to stay. It was near the station – not the best spot in town – but it had a double bed, a shower and a TV. And it was cheap.

I then decided to try and find out how to get a ticket for the game but was told that nothing would be available until tomorrow, one hour before kick-off.

★

That afternoon the England squad had a run out in the stadium. David Beckham and Robert Lee missed the training session, standing on the sidelines and reduced to taking the occasional light jog down one end of the pitch. Otherwise, it was the usual routine.

John Gorman was slinging balls around the field, Hoddle was mixing in with the players, proving he's as fit as the rest of them, and Clemence practised with the keepers.

I sat in one of the plastic orange seats provided for the press and watched Adams and Owen kick balls from one side of the field over to each other's chest on the other. Gorman kept an eye on the eighteen-year-old and every now and then shouted, 'Nice one, Michael. That's brilliant!'

Earlier on, Alan Shearer had given the captain's press conference to the regulatory bulk of inquisitive and weary writers. 'When it matters, England are there, fighting and giving everything,' he said at the start. The press, at last, had warmed to Shearer. They were starting to feel he was one of them, one of the boys. Let's not forget, he was still only twenty-seven. They treated an hour in the company of England's captain as a pleasure whereas once it had been a chore. They liked what he had to say. And he liked banging on about patriotism and flag-waving.

'We may not have the technique, but our hearts are big and brave,' he told us. 'When it comes to bravery we are as good as anyone in the world. In the dressing-room on Friday before the game against Colombia I could tell we were going to win. It was in the air. I told Glenn Hoddle as we went out, "We won't lose this." Against Argentina I expect it to be the same. We must set the tone of the game. We must go at them because that is what we are about.

'If we go out now, people will say we beat Tunisia, lost to the best side in the group and Colombia were not much. You can only beat what is put in front of you and that is why we are going to beat Argentina. It is important that England as a nation are seen to be beating one of the so-called big footballing countries, one of the World Cup favourites.

'There has been an expectancy hanging in the air since our European Championship victory over Holland. The people are willing us to do it and we can, we will. Our performance and victory over Holland opened people's eyes. We have no intention of closing them. When we do it, any doubts about us might just go away. By beating Argentina we can send out a message and that is "Believe in England".

'We want to win so much. Against Colombia on Friday we were arguing between ourselves. Paul Ince is not happy unless he is having a go at someone. He and I exchanged words. He wanted a forward to help out in midfield and I told him that Michael Owen was already there. He looked around and saw him and still had a go back at me. It is healthy.'

At the weekend Hoddle had spoken of the infamous Hand of God goal. He seemed to be keen to play down that incident, maybe in an attempt to maintain some calm on the terraces. Hoddle believed that if Maradona's first goal had been disallowed, he wouldn't have gone on to score that second wondrous goal that took him past six England players.

'Revenge is a horrible word,' the England coach said. 'Redress the balance is what I would say. I'm sure players like Peter Reid would love to be in the camp now. That goal stayed with us for a long time. For the football people in the country, we've got a chance of getting that result out of our system. I felt it was an injustice. It was a sickening blow we had to take. We couldn't believe how we went out.

'I never blamed Maradona. Not one of us did. The officials were the problem. Terry Butcher and I had to sit in the same room with Maradona doing the drugs test. I never felt any anger towards him. I shook hands with him on the pitch. I don't think Big Terry was in the same frame of mind.

'Maradona was the greatest player I've ever seen, better than Pelé. I saw him play when he was in Italy, where they put two men on him. As an individual talent, I don't think the world will ever see another player like Maradona. Pelé was a better team player but Maradona was better than anyone who has played football on this planet.'

Earlier on, the Argentina coach delivered a press conference and made the following statement: 'Our team has played very well at times, but it is very difficult for any team to be consistent. The English have a lot of style and dynamism and have some excellent players, especially in attack.

'I know Glenn Hoddle better as a player than as a coach. He was a very talented player with a lot of character, very wise on the pitch. As a coach, he has changed the English style of playing, making it more tactical, which has provided some excellent results, and consequently they have reached the second round.

'We can win this "classic" match as we have met England several times at this level. It's the hardest second-round match in the draw for both teams but this match has no political relevance, as you can't compare a football match to a war that took place in 1982.

'The match against England will be nothing like that of 1986. We want to be original. We won't "do a Maradona". We'll do our best to practise fair play.'

Shearer wasn't interested in talking of revenge either, but you couldn't be sure if he rated Maradona quite as highly as Hoddle did. 'People want to be able to say afterwards that the Hand of God thing is over,' he told the press. 'They want to talk about 1998, the day we beat Argentina. Only then can we talk of revenge. Let's not talk of history, only the future.'

Shearer claimed he wasn't bothered that he'd failed to get on the scoresheet after the opening game. 'I don't care if I don't get another one, just as long as we keep going.

'I thought the game against Colombia was my best performance so far. The system we played was enjoyable, chances were created and I'll have a bit more of that, thank you.

'But playing Argentina will be just like a game of chess. Both sides will be waiting for the other to make the first move.'

He was delighted with Hoddle's willingness to stick to the same team and added: 'The great thing about Michael Owen is that if eight or nine balls are hit over the defence then you know that sooner or later he will get on the end of one. David Beckham also gives you an attacking option with his free-kicks. He has a great range of passing as well.

'Argentina have not been tested yet. We are their biggest test. This, of course, is our biggest game, too. I have never played against them and I'm looking forward to it.'

But Shearer admitted he dreaded the prospect of golden goals in extra-time: 'We went through it in the European Championships against Spain and Germany,' he explained. 'It is nerve-wracking and no one wants to make the mistake that means you exit. Mind you, I wouldn't want to be the player to miss a penalty either.'

Shearer was a class act, a player's player. You could give him a back-slap now and wish him well in the game. This time last year your hand would have frozen on contact with him – either that, or he'd have punched your lights out.

As mentioned earlier, Henry Winter reckoned it was down to Shearer's tackle on Leicester City's Neil Lennon towards the end of the season which had caused much outrage in the tabloids. They had called for his head, some demanding he be dropped by

England or at the very least relieved of the captaincy. It was almost as though the papers where getting their own back after years of woeful interviews with the Newcastle forward.

Shearer had wondered why so many people slated his auto-biography when it was published and now he was getting a mauling in the press. Even Lennon said he wanted the matter dropped. Someone somewhere had told Shearer to start playing the game. 'Be yourself, Al, we'll all love you much better for it.'

★

After the players finished their workout Hoddle gave his final pre-match conference. The Argentinian and French interpreters stood to his right and David Davies hung about behind his left shoulder. A man straight out of *Miami Vice* compèred the proceedings. He had the moustache, the tan and the slick hands.

'A match against Argentina suits me better than one against Croatia, as we always play better against a stronger opponent,' were Hoddle's opening words. 'There's no particular stress on the staff or the players. For me, the pressure peaks during the first match, because if we lose, we have to chase after the others. We've got past this point and, as you saw during the training, we're all very relaxed. David Beckham and Robert Lee are a bit tired following the previous matches, and didn't join today's training, but they should be fit for tomorrow.'

Behind the TV cameras at the back of the room, a television monitor was showing the Germany *v* Mexico match. Hoddle showed how relaxed he was when he said, 'I think Germany just equalised.'

Asked for the umpteenth time about his relationship with David Beckham, Hoddle simply revealed the he and Becks had 'had words'. The player was now totally focused on the job at hand.

An Argentinian journalist asked Hoddle if he liked the idea of playing in an all-white strip. England had been due to play in red but the Danish referee, Kim Nielsen, was to wear that colour and FIFA refused to allow their refs to change strips.

'It's no problem,' replied Hoddle. 'I prefer to play in all-white. It was good for us in 1966 [England beat Argentina in the quarter-final wearing all-white] and I enjoyed many successful years at Spurs wearing all-white.'

Asked by a large-nosed Argentinian, who clearly fancied himself, if he could confirm the team line-up for tomorrow, Hoddle responded, laughing coolly, 'Yeah, *mañana*, *demain*, tomorrow, an hour before the match.'

But why not now, asked Beaky, irritated by Hoddle's flippancy. Who was this guy, some South American wiseguy?

'The present team is better than that of 1986, even if they lack experience,' Hoddle responded to a question from *The Independent*'s Glenn Moore. 'Look at the youngsters, Owen, Beckham, Scholes and Campbell. In four years' time they will develop their potential, and they could be the best team I've had anything to do with, as a player or as a manager.

'I've waited eighteen months to play David Beckham and Darren Anderton in the same team. ['So much for keeping the side quiet till kick-off,' muttered Henry Winter.] With David and Darren in the team, it gives us flexibility. Either can go wide and the balance of the team is right. It has been a long wait for me to play them together.

'I just hope that the team gets it right. In the end it's down to the players and how they feel. We've worked a lot on penalty-kicks, but we hope that it won't go that far.'

★

Out in the town I mingled with some of the supporters. I wanted to tell them that Owen and Beckham were starting. I wanted to instil faith and confidence in our boys. I felt we were going to win.

Sitting at a café, Jamie and Mark told me they hoped they hadn't come here for nothing. Wearing an England scarf and with a beer in hand, the two young Englishmen had left their hometown of Dorchester to start their 'World Tour' with the World Cup in France.

'We hitchhiked to Marseille, Toulouse and Lens and we had to save enough money to continue our trip to Sweden, the USA and Australia,' one of them told me. 'We don't have any tickets for the match but we're happy to be here and, giant screen or not, we'll watch England win from the Place Jean Jaurès [the town's main square].

'Hopefully there'll be a victory for England but in my opinion it'll come to penalties. Anyway, about the hooligans, closing the pubs isn't the answer, as anyone who comes to cause trouble will do so, regardless. St Etienne and its residents are like our own in Dorchester and we hope it all goes well.'

Carl Simpson, another England fan, showed me his home-made sign: '*Achète ticket pour le match Argentina-England*'. The French wasn't all it could be, but he was optimistic he'd get sorted. 'I came to France by minibus on 12 June. I went to Marseille, Toulouse and Lens. I really hope that I can buy a ticket for Tuesday night and I'm ready to pay up to about a hundred and fifty pounds. My friend bought his for two hundred.

'I think the decision not to show the game on the big screen is really unfair. The English fans are fed up of being punished because of the actions of the minority. And in relation to what happened in Marseille, we have to be objective: hooligans may be stupid, but the Tunisians played their part.'

The local shopkeepers were also hacked off with the town hall's decision to shut the place down early but realised the need to prepare for the worst. 'We've been told to shut at eleven o'clock and we won't take any risks,' one waiter told me. 'The slightest incident will close the restaurant. It's a shame that the match isn't being shown on the big screen on Tuesday as it penalises good fans. But in general, this World Cup has been good for us. Ninety-five per cent of our customers have been foreign, as locals prefer to stay at home in peace. The World Cup will have brought joy to St Etienne and it would be a great idea to permit concerts at the Place Jean Jaurès throughout the summer. It's good fun and it livens up the town.'

★

I left the square and settled in at my hotel. About half a dozen Argentinians were gathered in the foyer watching highlights of Germany's lucky escape against Mexico. A tall, thin lad wearing the nation's blue and white striped shirt grunted his acknowledgement at me. We had a broken conversation.

'Got a ticket?' I asked, distractedly, recalling those stories of Argie hooligans coming over the pond to beat up the English. The thought occurred that I might have stumbled upon the ringleaders. He waved a piece of paper in my face which I took to be a ticket.

Just then my best Argentinian pal in the world walked into the hotel foyer, lighting up one of her ridiculously strong foreign fags.

Marcela Mora y Araulo is the Argentinian football expert for the World Service, the *FT* and God knows where else. She drinks her whiskey neat – she prefers Irish, Bushmills if you've got it – and she's *always* working.

'How ya doing?' I said, excitedly.

'Good,' she replied, pursing the cigarette between her lips while juggling the enamel handle of the telephone that she'd been trying to work for the past minute. 'But how do I get out of this fucking hotel to somewhere where they can operate phones, take messages and, you know, do stuff that goes with running a decent joint?' she blurted out, furious that the phone wouldn't work. 'When did this message come in for me?' she asked the man behind the desk, holding out a wrinkled bit of notepaper.

He stares at her blank-faced.

'Come on!' she retaliated.

Marcela was waiting for a man from Sky News to contact her so he could arrange a time to do an interview the following morning. On top of that, her brothers had flown over from Argentina and wanted to meet up. She fired off some questions to the tall, thin fan in the foyer, gave the clerk a piece of her mind and took my arm, ushering me out of the hotel.

'Let's get a drink,' she said.

In the centre, after a taxi-driver reluctantly had taken us as near as he dared, we were met by a convoy of armoured police vehicles.

'Scum, vandals, bastards!' was the driver's view of the English.

The nine-hundred-strong police force had been bulked up to fifteen hundred. I reckoned they were all in the Place Jean Jaurès. Fans charged at the police but to me they didn't look English. They looked French. I spotted the Argentinian lad from the foyer and saw that he'd turned his shirt inside out. You could still make out the blue and white stripes but it made him less of a target.

The police were bashing the sides of their riot shields with massive truncheons that could've doubled up as baseball bats and were marching in a threatening manner towards the trouble-makers. All the shops and bars were shut and everyone was tense. Footie, eh?

We found a small bar that had braved the curfew and was still serving. 'Is it worth all this just for a bleedin' drink?' I asked Marcela.

'Come on,' she said. 'I'm starving.'

Strangely enough, the atmosphere in the bar was one of frivolity. The toilets had been smashed up and a porcelain basin lay on the floor in bits. There was a puddle in the men's and the ladies' was out of order. OUT OF ORDER! There was a bit of a queue.

At the bar was a bald, tattooed English alcoholic with one of those all-day tans that good alkies get. He claimed to be German. I reckoned he'd do anything for a drink except piss off. Behind him was a Scouser who was just laughing at the whole thing. Standing next to us was a man dressed up like an Austrian yodeller and carrying a guitar. My dictionary defines yodelling as: 'Singing with melodious inarticulate sounds and frequent changes between falsetto and normal voice in the manner of Swiss-mountain dwellers.' In other words, the behaviour of freaks who talk gibberish after a hard blow to the crown jewels. Do we attract these people or is St Etienne being run through by loonies, I wondered.

St Etienne closed down under a cloud. French yobbos had come in for a scrap and the Argies and English had left them to fight their own cops. I knew that in the morning the papers would say it was all our fault but for once, for one time only, I'm happy to report that this wasn't the case. Our boys were tucked up in bed. Tomorrow was going to be a long day.

CHAPTER FIFTEEN

The longest day

I woke early. My stomach was tied in knots and I felt sick with anxiety. The sun peered in through the window and told me to get my shit together. It had a big smile on its face, a big warm grin. It was happy and it bothered me.

After a blistering hot and cold shower – the only thing that worked round here was the power-shower – I nipped downstairs for breakfast.

Marcela was already at the stadium doing her interview for Sky News so I dined alone and watched the Argentinians wolf down scrambled eggs and a gallon of coffee. Did they *have* to smoke at this time of the morning?

At the self-service counter we nodded at each other with a sage-like countenance and spooned up seconds.

There was barely a murmur in the room. We were all too busy thinking. The game didn't start until 9 p.m. local time and already we were shitting bricks about it. The reality of just how tense this game had become was hitting home. I needed to get out of here. I needed to shift up to the ground. I needed to loosen the load.

In the press centre there was a small commotion when the foreign papers were delivered. Everyone wanted a copy to find out what the rest of the world's press were saying about the game. Why didn't they just ask each other?

I saw *The Sun* had gone for a picture of David Beckham in Madonna's frock with the headline: 'Don't Cry For Me Argentina'. Very imaginative. And they had 'Hand of Hod' props to poke up the Argies' noses. Where would we be without them?

Colette had arrived from Paris and I went to see if there was any chance of getting a match ticket. I'd almost forgotten I needed one. When you were this close to the stadium you reckoned you could just walk in, but it wasn't that simple.

She drew deeply on a cigarette, a bit like Chandler's Marlowe. She frowned and cursed and told me there were a few tickets going but that I'd have to wait. I felt that I could handle not getting in but the waiting was the thing that bothered me. The fear of not knowing. Uncertainty is a cruel curse.

I didn't fancy my chances of Colette sorting me out with a ticket but I had to keep hoping. If you didn't have hope, what did you have? The same could be said for the England team, but more and more pundits were saying they could do it.

The FA's official allocation of tickets for England supporters was just 2,049, the smallest amount so far. And there were more than twenty thousand England fans in this part of France.

The ground, known locally as 'The Cauldron', has a capacity of thirty-six thousand. More than ten thousand Argies were also expected to seek tickets. It was a mess.

The first ever meeting between Argentina and England took place at the 1962 World Cup in Chile. They played each other during the first round, when the English beat the Argentinians 3–1 before being knocked out in the quarter-finals by Brazil.

In the 1966 World Cup England beat Argentina in the quarter-finals 1–0. With Argentina winning the memorable 1986 quarter-final, England were 2–1 ahead in World Cup final victories. It was difficult to predict how this one was going to end.

Gabriel Batistuta was having a great day. On the eve of the match his wife Irina had given birth to their third son, Joaquin, in Florence, where Batistuta plays his club football. He was delighted, of course, and said, 'The best thing that could happen now would be to offer Joaquin the deciding goal against England.'

For others it was a more stressful morning.

★

John Sadler, 'the man who gives it to you straight', was standing next to me in the loos (you could bump into all sorts on the road in World Cup '98). He was as jittery as me. You'd be lucky to find a man who could piss straight today.

'I really fancy our chances if we can get past this lot,' he said.

I told him about the Argentinian fans in the hotel and described how nervous they'd been all morning.

'Really,' he said, surprised. 'Maybe it's getting to them, too.'

So there I was having a slash and a natter with *The Sun*'s venerable columnist and thinking about what I'd read in his paper that morning. Here are a few snippets:

'It is the mightiest match England have played in years and the consequences couldn't be more stark. Lose and they join the also-rans who have come down to earth at France '98 – but win and they can soar to the summit of world football.

'The other competing nations know the truth, too. If England overcome what is regarded by many as the best team in the tournament, they will earn the right to be rated as favourites.

'I join the optimism that says if they beat Argentina tonight, England will repeat the achievement of poor, stricken Sir Alf Ramsey thirty-two years ago and conquer the world.

'It is about time the rest of the world recognised English

163

technique and know-how – and tonight will tell them whether or not we have enough to beat the very best.

'Passarella, winning skipper in 1978, laid down the ground-rules when he took over [the Argentina team]. No long hair, no earrings and no homosexuals.

'England doesn't hope, it *expects* tonight. That Hoddle's team, built on judgement, faith and healing, can justify their manager's certainty that the best prepared side ever to leave our shores is on the threshold of historic triumph.'

Sadler had captured all the tension, expectation and drama in the build-up to the match. It can be difficult to like these guys but they certainly know how to bang the drum and get the nation going.

★

I had to keep moving. Reporters were coming into the canteen for lunch, smiling and laughing. They seemed to be handling the tension but I was cracking. I started drinking cans of beer. Christ, I'm turning into a hooligan, I thought. I felt like punching the bloke at the ticket desk. 'You'll have to wait like everyone else,' he told me. 'I don't care if you're English.'

Wanker.

I had to get out of that place. It was driving me nuts. I needed to meet some fans. *Take me to your leader, I feel like joining up.* The best place to do so struck me as being the centre of town, so I headed for the Place Jean Jaurès, which was packed with English people. The Union Jack was draped from the balconies above most of the bars and the big screen was on. A game of football was being played amongst the stray dogs and empty beer cans on the dirty orange dust that formed the pitch in the centre of the square.

Hot-dog stands were selling dodgy burgers for thirty-five francs a pop. Beer was forty-four francs a pint – that's nearly a fiver. As I strolled around I kept coming across blokes standing in pairs on street corners who'd come up to you with an inquisitive eye and a nose for the main chance. I caught tales of fans buying tickets down back alleys. The price ranged from £200 to £350. So far there had been no evidence of the six-hundred-pound prices I'd feared. I reckoned I'd be all right. I reckoned I'd get a few more beers in.

In the Café de Paris on one corner of the square I got chatting to JC, a Spurs fan, and his charming mate – I'm terribly sorry, I can't remember your name. He was a passionate Hammers fan with a dirty great big scar on his face and he'd got a smashing kid, he told me. Anyway, these two were drinking double vodkas and Coke like nobody's business and got the rounds in for me. I coughed up when I couldn't remember which Cup match it was that Christopher Wreh scored for Arsenal at Upton Park last season. That's right – Degs, is that your name? - journalists never pay their bets, but they do like a beer.

They were sorted for tickets – some swish hospitality packages, apparently – but the three lads from Luton who sat down next to us weren't so lucky.

'I'm well acquainted with your chairman,' JC told the Happy Hatters.

'Great,' replied the blond-haired fellow and we all had a drink.

Out on the street ticket prices were rising. The Luton boys had just been quoted two hundred and fifty pounds. More England fans were arriving in St Etienne by the hour.

'I know your chairman,' said JC to the Happy Hatters, slurring a little more this time, unsure if he was repeating himself.

They smiled politely and pointed out that he'd dropped his wallet. Match tickets and God knows what else fell on the floor on his way to the toilet.

JC returned to the table and thanked them all very much,

buying another round of drinks. He was bladdered. 'Did I mention I'm well acquainted with your chairman?' he enquired.

I left.

*

I cadged a lift back to the stadium with a group of official England supporters. They were very prim and proper and didn't take kindly to my songs about shoving it up the Argies. I think I might have drunk too much at lunch.

I got off early when the coach got stuck in a traffic jam, which was a shame because England's Official Supporters ended up having a pre-match snifter with the delicious Ulrika Jonnson, who had thankfully recovered from her night out with Collymore. *C'est la vie.*

I walked through a tight line of Argentinians. Typically, all the England fans were back at the pub while the South Americans were getting to the ground early. There was no malice. They were a noisy bunch, mind.

I could have got shifty about the Barras Bravas - the lads who'd vowed to slit the throat of every dirty *Engleesh* pig – but to be quite honest I got so caught up in the mêlée to get to the ground that it slipped my mind . . .

Looking back on it, I was lucky to have come out of St Etienne without a scratch. I was the only English person in the street. What was I doing there? The Friday night before, Argentinian fans had been blamed for a vicious attack on some bloke called Boris, an eighteen-year-old Croatian. They cut him with a knife from his mouth to his ear and shoved a broken wine bottle in his face.

Inside the Media Centre it was bleedin' chaos. There was a stack of journalists queuing up at the ticket desk. *Christ, is that the time!? I've got no chance of getting in there. Must force myself in.* Adam from

Loaded put a can of beer in my hand. The grumpy old git behind the desk asked if someone with a name not dissimilar to mine was there. 'Yep, I'm here!' I shouted.

'You're drinking,' he replied. 'Back of the queue.'

It was fucking hopeless. Journalists were practically fighting to get to the front of the desk, acting like old grannies at a jumble sale.

'Is Christian Smyth in here?' someone asked in a voice barely audible above the commotion.

I turned round and saw Paul from *Shoot* staring at me with a fat grin on his face and a large bloke standing next to him. In the bloke's hand were two tickets. For fifty quid I could have one. I could go to the ball. I was a happy chappy. That's how easy it was.

We tried to persuade a Peruvian radio journalist to buy the other ticket. I have no idea why we picked him. Fate chose him. His hair was curly in the fashion of Leo Sayer and he could have done with losing a few stone. He hesitated. What was his problem? *Buy the fucker and let's get our seats!* I couldn't hang about any more. I set off to the stadium. I couldn't believe I was there. I couldn't believe I'd got a ticket. For fifty quid!

Outside, a bloke from Liverpool noticed my accreditation pass and begged me for a ticket. You must be able to get one, he said. I remembered the dithering Peruvian and raced back to the media centre. The Liverpudlian had trouble keeping up. My adrenaline was pumping. I was buzzing. But there was nobody there. I couldn't spend too long looking because the game was about to kick off. No joy. I came back outside and gave the lad the bad news. He was crestfallen but said he appreciated the effort. I hope he was lucky.

I raced round to my side of the stadium. There were thousands of English fans packed high into this end of the ground. Loads of noise. *This is it, boys, this is the one!* England's official supporters' band were in the stands, trumpets and drums making a rumpus. This is my team and we're coming to get you, as Bobby Robson once said.

At the other end of the ground was the blue-and-white army but all I could hear was the thundering noise from our boys. I was in the corner, on the flanks. Two blocks up from the touchline, seat 190, row 9, block 34.

The Peruvian had made it. He sat there smiling when I got to our seats. He held up a microphone boom when a small group of Argentinians a few rows back started singing. How did he get that thing in to the stadium?

A posh-looking couple sat next to him. They were very smart, very old. I reckoned they'd taken a wrong turning on the way to the opera and for some reason ended up here.

On my left was an English chap and his son. I think they said they were from Yorkshire. I realised I was still pretty drunk. Then the teams came out.

★

The game kicks off. Seaman's down our end of the ground for the first half. Four minutes in and the Argentinian captain, Diego Simeone, has prodded the ball past him. He's not going anywhere as Seaman dives in but Simeone shows he can dive too. He crashes to the ground after catching the England keeper in the stomach. Penalty! I can't fucking believe it. The cheating wankers.

Batistuta blasts the ball into the back of the net, scoring for his new son just as he promised. I like Batistuta; he has a nobility about him, something that lifts him above the rest of his team-mates. He can eat at my table any time.

I'm pretty low. The Danish ref must have realised he's cocked up because he gives us a penalty almost immediately after Argentina score. Owen takes his first chance to run at the opposition and just about makes it into the box when Ayala cuts across him and he falls over. Hoddle said he wants Owen to go down and the boy's been listening. Waaa-hey! We're in for a cracker. Shearer converts. 1–1.

Ince gets a *yellow* card for arguing with the ref. He wants Ayala booked. Leave it out. Get on with the game. Argentina have conceded their first goal in this World Cup. Now they know they're in for a match.

Seven minutes later my world explodes. Beckham picks up the ball inside his own half and lobs it over to Owen who flicks it in front of him with his heel. Nice skill, that. The move takes him away from two Argentinian markers and into their half. The eighteen-year-old picks up pace and starts to run to his left, still heading for goal.

I'm on my feet. We're all watching in stunned silence. Then we roar. *Go on, Michael, go on, kid.*

Chamot and Ayala, two of the best defenders in the world, are left in Owen's slipstream as he takes off. He knows where he's going. He dips his shoulder and veers to his right, the ball stuck to his boot. Even Maradona would be proud.

For a moment it looks like Scholes might take the ball off his toe, but the United lad knows the score. Owen speeds past him, takes one look at where the keeper is and whacks the ball past him.

He's scored! He's fucking scored! The English fan and his kid to my left jump all over me. We cover each other in glory. The Peruvian is ecstatic. Even the old couple seem to appreciate something has happened. Something momentous.

Owen, you beauty, you little beauty. The Argentinians are stunned. What the fuck can they do about this kid? He's too strong. Too quick. Too damn good.

England are all over them. Ince lets fly a cheeky thirty-yard shot that dips over the bar. Scholes misses a sitter (again!) in the thirty-eighth minute. Adams and Campbell are sweeping up at the back.

Ortega, Argentina's brilliant number 10, does enough to win a free-kick on the edge of the area. It must be half-time soon. England seem to be taking too long to organise the wall. Then, in a flash, Veron slips the ball down the right-hand side of the defenders to Zanetti who had wheeled off the edge of the box and makes room to blast a shot past Seaman. It's a clever free-kick and a good goal, but we deserve a better score-line. The whistle goes for half-time. 2–2.

I phone the lads in the pub back home. 'Come on, you Prince's Head!' I shout. I can hear the TV and the roar of beer orders. They're watching me watching the best match of the World Cup so far. Weird.

I finish my call and go back to my seat. The game's already restarted but there's something not quite right. 1, 2, 3, 4, 5, 6, 7, 8, 9, 10 . . . there are only ten England players on the pitch. Who's missing? What's happened?

The Peruvian motions with his arms, waving them above his head in a twirling fashion that Manuel the waiter would be familiar with. 'He go crazy,' he tells me.

'Who?' I ask.

'Meester Beckham,' replies the Peruvian.

'Beckham!' I cry.

'He's been sent off,' says the bloke from England.

I can't believe it. I'm stunned. I was only away for a few minutes. He can't be. He's never been sent off. I'm blabbing. I'm speechless.

The England fans start clapping. The trumpet-player breaks into the opening bars of *The Great Escape*. They know what to do. It's backs to the walls, boys. Take no prisoners. Every man to the pumps. Woman and children go first. This is no ordinary drama.

The scumbag Argies, the cheating bastards, they shouldn't be in this game. We were all over them first half. Now they've got one more man. Well, just try it, sunshine. Just you try it. Adams and Campbell are ready for anything. Shearer drops on to the wing and Owen stays up front on his own. We're going to do you on the counter. Later we wonder why Owen didn't go on the wing. He's got the pace. Shearer could hustle up front, he's the best at holding up the ball. But there's little time for that.

Hoddle reorganises the ten men left. Southgate comes on for Le

Saux and Merson comes on for Scholes. I'm pleased that the Merse, after all he's been through, gets a World Cup appearance under his belt, but surely McManaman would have been the player to bring on. His pace and understanding with Owen could have been vital.

Adams and Campbell baton down the hatches and there's no getting past them. Campbell has a goal disallowed when the linesman spots Shearer elbowing the keeper. I'm cringing on the sidelines. The crowd are baying for blood. The nonstop singing and clapping to *The Great Escape* is making my throat dry. Even the old French couple are clapping along, supporting our boys.

The whistle blows. We've made it to extra-time, golden goals. I can't take much more of this. The Argentinians at the other end of the ground are stunned. The English fans at our side just keep singing. We've survived forty-five minutes a man down and we'll get through another thirty minutes of golden goals in extra-time.

And now it's down to penalties. The tension is too much to bear. When Ince misses his shot the whole crowd seem to stamp their feet in a jungle-drum rhythm. *'Doon dun dun, doon dun dun, doon dun dun INCE!'* He acknowledges the crowd's respect. He really shouldn't be taking penalties but he wants to make up for not taking one at Euro '96.

When Batty misses, I'm stunned. Shocked. Speechless. I sit down. I stand up. I don't know what I'm doing. *Why us? Why can't we win one of these things?*

I turn to the English pair to my left and they're in tears. The young lad's clinging on to his dad, unable to look at the players on the pitch. The French couple sit motionless. The singing stops and not even the band can get a tune going.

I feel like I'm in a bubble. I can hear sounds around me but I'm detached from it all. I feel like I've been robbed, like I should have seen it coming.

As the crowd get up from their seats and slowly shuffle towards the exits, I hear one idiot say, 'Let's trash St Etienne!'

Everyone turns on him and I hear one woman scold him: 'We don't need that kind of talk, that kind of rubbish here!'

Suitably humiliated, he slinks off. These people are cowards, scum. They only do things in a mob. If the decent fans turns on them, we can get rid of the hooligans.

Which force is more powerful – decency and principles or an overweight, blotchy beered-up slob? In any other circumstances these people would be laughed at. Or we'd give them our spare change, dismissing them as down-and-outs.

Tonight is not the time for violence, not after the bravery of our boys on the pitch. There had been one moment when the crowd had separated after the opening goal, as if trouble was brewing, but the drama was too intense. We were there to watch football. If you don't like it or you want to cause trouble, why don't you just piss off.

★

In the media centre (I didn't know where else to go) I waited for Hoddle to deliver his press conference. I wouldn't have blamed him if he'd got the first plane out of France *but staying to face the music is the manager's lot*, isn't it?

Hardened pressmen wandered around the place in a spin. They had to deliver the biggest story of the World Cup but couldn't believe what they'd seen. A game with everything. Except the right result.

Below are the responses of the players and the management. I don't want to dwell on the game. It's too dispiriting. How must Beckham be feeling? How must Owen be? How can you score a goal like that and end up losing? Life really isn't fair.

Batistuta and Veron spoke for the Argentinians: 'Coming off during the game doesn't bother me and meant nothing,' said

Batistuta of his substitution. 'Our aim was simply to win. We were patient and this qualification is really fantastic for us. When I scored a goal, I did not for one moment think about my personal ambitions. In our team, it doesn't matter who scores; the important thing is to win. Our aim is to get to the finals and not worry about who our opponents will be.'

Veron was thrilled: 'We are happy to get through to the next round, both for ourselves and for the people of Argentina. But life goes on and we must keep a cool head. We scored quickly but the other team soon pulled ahead and it was very difficult to equalise. We were aiming for victory but, with the English on the defensive, the match didn't seem winnable. Our never-ending battle was finally rewarded.'

There was no mention by either of them of the great part the England team had played in the game. Or the fact that Argentina had been outplayed for just about the whole of the first half. Or that England had had more chances.

Coach Passarella was more charitable: 'The match tonight against England was very open, especially when they had to play with only ten men. From that moment on they played defensively and counter-attacked. They showed themselves to be a very solid and strong team with two outstanding strikers.

'Our set-piece goal was perfectly prepared by Veron; Zanetti, who controlled the ball well, knows how to conclude a free-kick successfully.

'England played in a typical English way, a very solid team. Even though they lost one player, we were always struggling. This was undoubtedly the toughest second-round game so far. As for our next opponent, Holland, we have already studied them on tape.'

★

When Glenn Hoddle finally came out to face us, he was a forlorn fellow. He had been in the players' dressing-room for some considerable time and he had changed and was ready to make a brief statement.

'Tonight's result is disappointing for England,' he said. 'We knew that the match against Argentina would be tough but we were hoping that it would be our night.

'We can't put all the blame on David Beckham; we handled ourselves very well without him. The players gave everything they had, the whole team played really well. The whole country can be very proud of their performance. With eleven against eleven, the match would have been quite different. After equalising, my players' football got much better.

'You can't force someone to take a penalty; I asked David Batty if he wanted to take it and he accepted. Losing is very hard to take, but we have to look to the future. We have some lessons to learn from this match, as we had some problems with our concentration.

'It's a very strange emotion to end with, losing on penalties. To lose like this is always very hard. We wish Argentina good luck for the rest of the tournament.' And with that he was gone.

In the mixed zone, disconsolate England players had to run the gauntlet of journalists in order to get out of the stadium. Everyone wanted a piece of David Beckham but only the following players spoke to the press:

David Seaman: 'We did what we could, and it was a performance in itself to have played a man down for such a long time, without being too tired. It was a very difficult match and we were really unlucky. It's a shame it had to go to penalties.'

Gareth Southgate: 'We played very positively, but unfortunately we were one man down on the pitch. I'm really disappointed to have lost. As for David Beckham's red card, don't worry, he's fine. We are friends and we are going to go out together this evening all the same. I'm sure that tomorrow will be a very sad day. But we have to look ahead: the team is put together with young, promising players. It's sad to lose like this, but we needn't be ashamed as we showed the team's true potential.'

David Batty: 'We were worked up during the match. After the [Argentinians'] penalty, we stayed positive. Personally, I feel a bit cheated by the result. It's a big disappointment for the whole team as we played really well. It was very difficult playing ten against eleven, but that's when we had the most chances in midfield to recover the ball and cause problems for the Argentine defence.'

Gary Neville: 'I haven't yet watched the replay so I can't say whether the refused goal [by Campbell] was fair. It's terrible to lose on a penalty shoot-out, especially as we played really well. It was very difficult to continue after David Beckham was sent off, but we were lucky Michael Owen scored a fantastic goal. At eighteen, he's a very gifted player. As for Argentina, they'll be difficult to beat and could well get through to the finals.'

Darren Anderton: 'We showed that we can play very well and this is what we did tonight. It's a shame, because now we have to go home. Michael Owen wanted to be a very good player, but today shows that he is fantastic. I am very disappointed. You always feel that way when you lose after a penalty shoot-out.'

Paul Merson: 'We played very well and everyone gave their best. With only a ten-man team, we didn't think it was a handicap and all in all, I'm satisfied despite our defeat. In fact we could have played even longer without being able to score. One small regret, however: in my opinion the two penalties were not justified, while the referee could have given a penalty against the hand-ball committed by an Argentinian. Congratulations to Argentina, but they haven't won yet. Owen is an exceptional player and he scored a goal that was out of this world.'

★

It's two hours after England have been knocked out of France '98 and I'm walking back into St Etienne. Elsewhere there are sporadic outbursts of trouble but no one bothers me. It's as if I'm floating away from the scene of a crime. We were robbed tonight but I can't quite work out who is to blame.

England's World Cup began with acts of savageness and it's ended in a flood of tears and broken hearts, but also with a sense of hope for the nation that gave football to the world.

In this encounter with Argentina the work put in by the defence at times conjured up images of Rorke's Drift, but the lasting impression will be the smile on a teenager's face after he danced past the world's best to score a goal of sublime majesty and beauty that will live long in the memory of those of us who were lucky enough to witness it at first hand tonight.

It's not much to hold on to when you're walking home in the dead of night with rampaging locals on the look-out for Brits *to beat up* and defeat staring back at you like a double-barrelled shotgun.

But it's enough.

CHAPTER SIXTEEN

Tee hee and sympathy

I stood on the platform waiting for the slow train to take me from St Etienne to Lyon where I'd catch the TGV back to Paris. It was another sunny, hot day in the mid-south of France. But bugger that.

I spotted a Labour MP, bald, middle-aged and from the north, on the phone to his secretary rescheduling appointments for that afternoon back in England.

Archie MacPherson and Trevor Steven were sitting near by, Steven kicking stones off the side of the platform. I sat down next to them and whipped out my copy of *L'Equipe*. Trevor Steven, who played in the 1986 Hand of God match, looked dejected. *I can't believe it's happened again*, his expression said.

Three England fans walked up and down the platform with heavy, bulging rucksacks on their backs. One of them pulled up alongside Archie and asked if they could have their photo taken with the *Eurosport* boys.

England were packing up and shipping out. For us, the war was over.

The headlines in *L'Equipe* heaped praise on the match and on Michael Owen in particular. They had devoted their front page to a picture of the Liverpool prodigy slipping past Chamot to score that wondrous goal. The caption said that the young Owen is one of the heroes in a superb evening and extraordinary match. He is a star. '*Quelle soirée!* – What a night!'

Le Monde was even more gushing: 'The extraordinary little blond with cleancut looks, the model of a well-behaved young man who has everything to make his parents, coaches and country proud of him . . .'

A series of tributes to last night's performance graced the pages of the paper: 'It was a marvellous night, the match was excellent, we couldn't have asked for a better scenario, it was truly a final come early,' said Michel Thiolierre, mayor of St Etienne.

'We're really disappointed. That's the third big international meeting we've lost on penalties and it's infuriating. Argentina were really very good and we're not ashamed to lose to them,' said Keith Wiseman, president of the FA.

'We're very disappointed and Argentina were too good when we went down to ten men. We could have won the penalties but didn't have any luck,' said Bobby Charlton.

'Bravo, it was really superb, the atmosphere was very friendly. Unfortunately it's over in St Etienne. Moreover, I'm very disappointed that England lost by so little. It was a really exceptional match,' said Arsène Wenger.

'It's a shame that the English were down to ten. The first half was exceptional. It was a great match between two superb teams and without doubt it was the best of the World Cup so far,' said former French coach Michel Hidalgo.

The fans seemed to be united in their criticism of Beckham. *He cost it for us. No one likes a smart-arse.* That sort of thing.

We were not yet aware that a psychotic English fan had stabbed a man to death. Everyone on the train back to Paris was depressed, tired and quiet. The England fan, who looked remarkably similar to a bloke I saw on the train from St Etienne to Lyon, apparently stabbed a fellow passenger who he thought was a) smiling at him and b) an Argentinian on the night of the match. Madness!

Once we reached Paris, I went from the Gare du Lyon to Montparnasse station and from there to La Baule for a final conference with Hoddle. I noticed there were fewer gendarmes at the station to greet our train, as if the fear of English hooliganism had disappeared with our elimination from the tournament.

★

In La Baule the air hung heavy. We had a job to do and there was the whiff of smoke clearing. It seemed appropriate that we were camped up in the forest of Escoublac.

Hoddle made a statement: 'I'm still convinced that if we had got over the Argentina obstacle it would have given us the confidence to go far. Unfortunately, we will never know the potential of our team, which really upsets me. I always thought we had a chance to win this match, even when our team was reduced to ten against eleven.

'Michael Owen scored one of the most beautiful goals of this World Cup. He has an exceptional talent. I'm very proud of our performance – we didn't deserve to lose.

'In the changing-rooms after the match the players were really emotional. David Beckham was particularly disappointed – he didn't say anything, he just sat alone, lost in thought. He made a foolish mistake but I don't think he deserved a red card. He's going to have to live with it and learn something from it. I'm not too worried about him because he has a strong character. He's young and has a promising future. I hope the fans are fair to David, that he doesn't become the scapegoat of our elimination. No one is to blame.

'We haven't shown enough concentration in this tournament and we're paying for it now. From now on we're all going to have to deal with this loss. At this level the slightest lapse of attention is unpardonable. You saw this when we played Romania in the first round and even more so when we played Argentina, when their 2–2 equaliser, just before half-time, could have been avoided if we'd concentrated just a little more.

'It's true that this is the third consecutive time that we've missed out on making it in a major competition on a penalty shoot-out. It is difficult to put your finger on the reason for these repeated losses, but the psychological side and the fact that in the past they've gone against us are definitely parts of it.

'As coach, my disappointment is even greater than it was as a player in the 1986 World Cup – I have a broader view of things now. Now we have to concentrate on the 2000 European Championship.'

Asked whether the team might have practised a few more penalties, given their history, Hoddle was sceptical. 'I'm not denying practice does help,' he said. 'A golfer can practise a thousand putts on the putting green. But he can then go out on the last day of a tournament when there are thirty thousand spectators watching and miss it. If it was all down to practice, and it always went in for you, then it would be a simple scenario. It isn't like that.

'We do practise them. David Seaman has practised saving them. But it is on that walk from the halfway line to the penalty spot that a player knows whether he is going to miss it or not. You can't force someone to take one. David Batty and Paul Ince said they wanted to take a penalty. When you get a positive vibe from a player like that, you've got to go with it. The five who took them were up for it.

'Too many things go through your mind if you keep losing at penalties. If you keep winning them, like the Germans, then psychologically you feel that it is going to go your way. The confidence is there. That is why we sent everyone up we possibly could on set-plays during the golden-goal period because our record on penalties has not been fantastic. It's just a mental thing. Germans keep winning them.'

Perhaps that was what Hoddle meant when he said that Eileen Drewery, the woman he believed had healing hands, could have improved England's chances by twenty per cent. She could have pumped up the boys' self-belief before the shoot-out.

But how would people react to the sight of this little old lady, the pub landlady who rejuvenated Hoddle's playing career after injury, pottering onto the field like Barbara Windsor in *EastEnders* to give 'her boys' one last lift?

Let's face facts. Argentina, like Germany, practise their penalties, running a competition at the end of each training session to alleviate the tedium of running and ball skills. All bar one of the Argentinian penalties was dispatched with the calmness and authority that comes from practice.

David Beckham practises his free-kicks every day. That's why he scores so many. It's simple. What was Hoddle wittering on about, saying practice doesn't make perfect? This, remember, is the man who thought Owen wasn't a natural goalscorer.

When Michael Owen raced past Chamot and Ayala to score, Paul Merson turned to Owen's club team-mate, Steve McManaman, on the bench and said: 'He won't be playing for you next season. If I was an Italian club owner,' continued Merse, 'I would give Liverpool a blank cheque for him. From what I've seen, he's better than Ronaldo. Argentina's defenders are terrified of him.'

While it has been proved that Owen's staying on Merseyside, he is now insured for £60 million by Liverpool FC and valued at more than £30 million. 'He would have become even more known worldwide if we'd have continued in this tournament,' agreed Hoddle. 'That's the sad thing.'

But Owen has time on his side. He could still play in at least three more World Cups. He can carry on at Anfield where Steve Heighway, the youth-team coach, has played such a pivotal role, and he can pick and choose his time to travel abroad when he feels like it. In ten years' time, if he likes.

David Beckham released a public apology in *The Sun*. The paper seemed to have become the official voice for English football. Even the manager aired his opinions in their pages. Football's take on money-laundering, I wondered?

Beckham poured out his heart to *The Sun* the day after the defeat. The nation was gutted but not, it seemed, half as gutted as Beckham, who must have busted a gut to write so many words in such a short space of time. It was without doubt the worst moment of his career. Like we didn't know that.

Beckham wanted England supporters to know that he was deeply sorry. England supporters wanted Beckham to know exactly what they thought of him. Gallows humour was sweeping the nation and it was the United player's head that was in the noose.

After he had been sent off, Beckham returned to the dressing-room and sat, feeling sick and numb. He then went to stand in the tunnel to watch the rest of the game, the tension of the penalty shoot-out and the aftermath. It was hard to stomach, particularly as Beckham knew he would have been one of the penalty-takers. He felt he'd let the side down and apologised to each and every one of them as they sat in silence after the match. It was Tony Adams who broke the silence: 'Well done everybody, you couldn't have done more.'

Beckham was lucky to have his family at the ground and later managed to ring Victoria Adams in America. She'd been watching the game and was crying down the phone.

'After leaving the stadium, we all went back to our hotel where we had a quiet drink together. Many of the lads stayed up all night – I went to bed at around 5.30 a.m.'

Beckham's contrition was complete.

★

The England squad flew back to Heathrow on July 1 on board a Concorde specially provided by British Airways. Owen waved a flag out of the cockpit as proud fans cheered their boys home. It was a strange way to end the whole thing. We'd lost a match but regained some dignity and pride on the world stage.

It was over.

CHAPTER SEVENTEEN

The final verdict

So in the end we went as far as Paraguay and a little further than Iran. Thus were the sentiments of Danny Baker who took England's demise in the World Cup as a cue to bleat on about his mate Gazza, and what a difference he'd have made.

'We all know Gazza can hack a big-time penalty shoot-out,' opined the lardy *Times* columnist. 'So why not take him instead of Ferdinand or Lee?'

Well, Gazza might have managed a trot up the pitch to place the ball for a penalty-kick, but he was in no fit state for running around a full-sized pitch for half an hour. Even Sunday League players take it easy the night before.

That England exited the World Cup earlier than their ability merited cannot be doubted. That they displayed Corinthian spirit and skill in the face of daunting expectation is similarly undeniable.

The fact is they had little of the luck necessary to carry sides through the duration of a Cup competition and suffered at least three debatable decisions from a Danish referee who, like the fellow who refused to send off Ronald Koeman the last time England were dumped out of World Cup football, seemed to give everything to the opposition.

It was hardly David Beckham's fault that we failed in France. Nor can we put it down to the absence of Paul Gascoigne, Matthew Le Tissier, Dennis Wise or any of the other tricksters who might have improvised something out of nothing on that night in St Etienne.

Beckham was foolish (this seems to have become the adjective of choice to describe the incident) and he let England down. But come on — lifting a leg against an Argentinian is a bit like a dog cocking his rear peg against a tree. It's just something you do.

The Argentinian captain was booked for his foul on the Manchester United maestro and the ref should have left it at that. Alex Ferguson was spot on when he said: 'What David did was foolish and unprofessional. Although the little backward flick of his foot which he aimed at Diego Simeone wouldn't have broken an egg and should never have been a red-card offence, he has to live with the damage his action did to England's chances of reaching the quarter-finals of the World Cup.

'But the way he was treated by sections of the media afterwards makes you wonder if the attitudes to sport in our country have gone totally insane.'

Ferguson revealed that Beckham had run into referee Kim Nielsen before in the away leg of Manchester United's European Cup quarter-final with Porto in March 1997. 'Beckham was caught up in an off-the-ball incident and should have been booked,' said Ferguson, adding that on that occasion the ref let him off with a lecture. 'When the trouble occurred in St Etienne, Nielsen may have thought, "I gave you a break once and you don't seem to have learned from it — so this time you're off."'

And what about the players that stayed on the pitch?

In Adams and Campbell we saw two defensive performances that will stand alongside those of Moore, Hunter and Charlton. Every time the tricky Ortega began to thread passes into the path of Batistuta and Veron, there was Adams, legs outstretched, cutting off the supply. His positional play and leadership from the back were outstanding. For me, he was the man of the match in St Etienne.

Sol simply had an awesome World Cup. His domination of Tunisia, where he swatted forwards aside like flies, and that run against Colombia where he stormed upfield like a thundering wildebeest were enough to ensure his place in the team of the tournament (alongside Chelsea defender Marcel Desailly). But the all-round control against Argentina, the authority he showed against one of the world's best strike-forces and *that* goal. Oh, that goal that should have been given. Well, say no more, Sol, you did us proud.

Those boys can look back on their work in France and think, 'Blimey! We did all right.'

I thought Rio Ferdinand had a storming World Cup even if only a few of us got to see it. His ball skills, calm manner and willingness to get stuck in during training were, for me, one of the highlights of France '98. He looked a real class act, and perhaps one of Hoddle's best decisions (which will ultimately benefit English football) will prove to be the moment he surprised us all and elected to take Rio along for the ride. The experience the West Ham *libero* will have gained on this trip will be invaluable, and a defensive partnership of Sol and Rio at the next World Cup is a juicy proposition.

In midfield Paul Ince showed that, when it comes to the big games, he is still the man for the occasion. Constantly badgering (I put it politely) his team-mates on the field, off it he was a charmer. Smiling, laughing, having a good time. He has become a role model for a generation. West Ham fans should give him a break.

Likewise Alan Shearer. Gone is the dour northerner, the man who treated the press like pariahs and had two good words for a reporter. *No. Comment.* From the moment he got off the plane, the England captain was willing to lead the line, get stuck in at press calls, have a laugh, chuck in a few harmless indiscretions – you know, stuff that makes a man interesting. He has mellowed. (Sometimes you forget he's still only twenty-seven.)

It was great to see Paul Merson get a taste of World Cup football after all he's been through. Anyone who's read his autobiography *Rock Bottom* will be amazed that this man was anywhere near France '98 and it is a tribute to Merse, his friends and family that he has pulled himself out of the pit. Glenn Hoddle obviously has a thing about character and role models. Take note, Mr Baker. In the modern world you need athletes to compete on the football field, not comedians.

In Michael Owen, England have their first genuine superstar since, well, since Bobby Charlton. It's hard for us English to comprehend what that means but let's put it this way. In Keegan, Gazza, Robson and so on, we had players who were good but not necessarily the best in the world. In Owen we have someone who will, without question, be the best and most feared striker in the world, if not now then in a couple of years' time. Hoddle seems hardly able to believe his luck at having such a prospect. 'It's an exciting feeling,' he said in his summing-up of the England effort in France, 'when you think of Shearer and Owen still being young enough to perform together for another four years.

'Michael is a great player and he's going to be an even better one. I don't think it's right to make comparisons: it's difficult to compare Ronaldo with Pelé, for instance, because their styles of play are different. Then again, Maradona was different from anyone I've ever seen.'

So who would you say Michael's like?

'There isn't anyone, so let's make him unique. Let's say he's got a special talent. He's got wonderful pace – I've not seen anyone run faster with the ball since I first saw Ryan Giggs at sixteen – and he's got an intelligence to run without the ball, to make runs off the ball. That is his major, major strength. He's got a great mind.'

Hoddle maintained his argument that he was right to 'nurse' Owen's entrance into the World Cup. 'How I wanted to start him in the tournament I believe was right,' he said. 'If he'd have gone in in the first game – the most important one – and we'd had a dodgy result and he hadn't scored, people would have been saying he was too young and shouldn't have been thrown in at the deep end. So we nursed him in, and we were always going to do that.

'He's done a magnificent job while he's been here in the World Cup but something tells me the boy wants to learn. The other day he said to John Gorman, "I can't believe how I stretch now!" His agility work is so much improved.

'He's done a lot of gym work with us on a couple of areas where he's weak. He needed to strengthen parts of his upper body, and he's worked really hard in the gym. There's a lot of things there that I just see him willing and wanting to learn off the pitch and on it to become a better player.

'He still needs to learn a lot, and he'll learn that himself as he plays at the top level. The greatest teacher is yourself when you are playing at the highest level, and he's a lad who thinks about his game and wants to improve. I think he'll take all he's learned out here and use it next season. If we keep seeing an improvement in him, he's going to be a wonderful, wonderful asset.

'I don't think there is anyone else in the world of his age I'd rather have in my side. If there had been anyone as good at his age, they'd have been here at this tournament. He's shown the maturity of a twenty-four or twenty-five-year-old and his pace is electrifying. If we had gone on here, who knows what he could have achieved? But what he has achieved will only give him even more confidence to do it time and time again for his club and for his country.'

And so to the manager. There is only one man who can shoulder the blame for our untimely exit, even if it was spectacular in its drama. Hoddle has said that what saddened him most about the defeat with Argentina wasn't the penalties, the red card or the iffy calls made by Nielsen. No, it was the conviction that, if ten men could snuff out Argentina, an irresistible tide of self-belief and 'destiny' would embrace his squad and take them all the way. There were many who'd agree with that prognosis, myself among them, but the fact is we didn't do ourselves any favours by fielding a weak side against Romania, thus ensuring we had to compete in the tougher half of the draw.

Hoddle appears to be a man who takes opinions and criticism of his work with the stoicism and good humour of a grumpy news-agent, irritated when his shop gets overrun with schoolchildren. Hoddle fills up his spare time by working in the media like the proprietor stacks his shop with sweets. It's just the journalists (kids) he can't stand. If the sniping that's already started carries on we'll have signs reading 'No more than two journalists at a time' posted up outside England press conferences in future.

It does him no favours to deride the opinions of those who spend their lives following the game, writing about its highs and lows.

If you've got eyes and a brain you can work out what football's all about. As my old man used to say, 'Twenty-two men kicking a cow's bladder round a park — it's not exactly rocket science, is it?' Hoddle may choose to surround himself with sycophants who treat his theories on fitness, training routines and diets as if he's the messiah, spreading the word, but as the man himself said, all he's doing is making English players give up stuff they've been accustomed to doing for a quarter of a century. It's not *that* big a deal.

Three of the four goals England conceded in the tournament were judged by Hoddle to have been caused by lapses in concentration. Nobody in particular was to blame; they were just, *malheureusement*, something that comes with the English game. 'You get away with these things in the Premiership,' he said after the Argentina game. But such a statement hides a failure to accept two things. First, that as the tournament wore on, it became clear that Graeme Le Saux was less a defender and more a winger who could track back — a role he had played earlier in his career. That Le Saux suited Hoddle's requirements for a player who could switch from 3–5–2 to 5–3–2 there was no doubt. Le Saux's problem was that he was hopeless in defence.

Hoddle ejected left-sided players like Andy Hinchcliffe because in the final build-up to France '98 he failed to meet the manager's demands to track back from one end of the pitch to the other.

In Georgia at the start of Hoddle's reign, the Italian press said of Hinchcliffe and his role in the team: 'This is technically as tight an England team as we've ever seen. We should not underestimate the value to this team of Hinchcliffe. We read in the English press that you don't think much of his skill, but he is as important as any other player when the England team are in possession of the ball because he holds the shape of the team. Crucially on that left side, he allows the team to function. It comes from Hinchcliffe.'

Hoddle seemed to treat a defender's ability to defend as a bonus. His main requirement was that such players could cross the ball and do as he told them. Dogmatic, but hardly practical given the dearth in defensive talent in our country.

To compound this positional problem, Hoddle left Phil Neville, a former England Schoolboys captain and more than capable left-sided player, at home.

When things go wrong, the coach explains it in a way that exempts him from any blame. It doesn't work in the press and, increasingly, it doesn't wash in the dressing-room.

Then there were the tactical decisions on the pitch. Why bring on Merson instead of McManaman when the Argentinians had already shown they didn't like whippy Liverpool players running at them? Why not reunite the prodigy and his pal? Why was Shearer switched to the right wing when Owen could have been allowed to run from there like he had, more or less, on his début back at Wembley against Chile?

And then there were the penalties. Hoddle replaced Le Saux, who was cracking under the pressure, with Southgate and brought on Merson for the industrious Scholes in extra-time. Gary Neville admitted afterwards: 'About five minutes from the end of extra-time I was looking around the pitch and thinking, "I can't see any penalty-takers out here." Apart from Alan Shearer, Michael Owen and Paul Merson, I didn't see anybody in the team who would even be a substitute penalty-taker with their club.'

David Batty raised his hand and advanced as a penalty-taker because that's the sort of man he is. He's proud and he's from Yorkshire. Like Goughy, Trueman and Boycott, he'd die for his country – so what if he hadn't taken a penalty since his sixteenth birthday?

Hoddle should have known his players, should have realised why Batty was up for it. He should have recognised his player's limitations. He said later that he didn't want the game to go to penalties because England weren't mentally equipped to deal with them. So why bring on a defensive player when there were other options on the bench? *Why? Why? Why?*

Batty said he was sure he knew how to come back from the missed penalty. 'I won't let it haunt me,' he said on the way back to La Baule after the match. 'I think I'm a strong personality and I refuse to let my last kick of the World Cup play on my mind. I'm not going to make a joke out of it, but I'm also not going to be destroyed by it.'

In this era of low alcohol and high fibre, stretching, massage and faith-healers, Batty took the spot-kick that decided our fate in the biggest tournament in the world because he felt like it.

After the match, the morgue-like atmosphere in the England dressing-room was broken by Hoddle. His manner and display of emotion surprised the senior players who wondered if Hoddle's ice-cool veneer would ever be broken. Walk from the stadium with pride, he told them. You have served your country well and done everything that was asked of you.

It was the middle of the night when the England party finally checked in to their hotel in La Baule. Some went to the bar and began the inquest while others got no sleep at all. For England, their longest day was over.

Hoddle said this was the best prepared squad to have ever left these shores but then failed to spend much more than a modicum of time practising the skill that had caused our exit from the last two major tournaments we'd got far in.

Then, rather bizarrely, he suggested that with 'Come On' Eileen on board, England might have improved by twenty per cent. There are those among us who wonder if the man is playing with a full deck.

With a contract that takes him up to Euro 2000 and the possibility of an extension to the next World Cup, the jury is out. The sword hangs over Hoddle's head like it has done above all England managers before him. His employers at the FA seem to be satisfied with the job he did at France '98 and look forward to greater things in Holland in two years' time.

As for the rest of us . . . Well, to recall what David Walsh wrote during the first-round stages in the *Sunday Times*: 'Our thumbs are neither up, nor down. Merely delicately poised.'